Rick Steves'

Best of
GREAT BRITAIN

*Make the Most of Every Day
and Every Dollar*

**John Muir Publications
Santa Fe, New Mexico**

Originally published as *2 to 22 Days in Great Britain*

Other JMP travel guidebooks by Rick Steves
  Asia Through the Back Door (with Bob Effertz)
  Europe 101: History, Art, and Culture for the Traveler
    (with Gene Openshaw)
  Mona Winks: Self-Guided Tours of Europe's Top Museums
    (with Gene Openshaw)
  Rick Steves' Best of the Baltics and Russia (with Ian Watson)
  Rick Steves' Best of Europe
  Rick Steves' Best of France, Belgium, and the Netherlands
    (with Steve Smith)
  Rick Steves' Best of Germany, Austria, and Switzerland
  Rick Steves' Best of Italy
  Rick Steves' Best of Scandinavia
  Rick Steves' Best of Spain and Portugal
  Rick Steves' Europe Through the Back Door
  Rick Steves' Phrase Books for: German, Italian, French,
    Spanish/Portuguese, and French/German/Italian

Thanks to my eternal travel partner, research assistant, and wife, Anne. Thanks also to Roy and Jodi Nicholls, and Dave Hoerlein for their research help, to our well-traveled readers for their input, and to the British friends listed in this book who make a visit to Britain so much more than a series of palaces, museums, and Big Bens.

John Muir Publications, P.O. Box 613, Santa Fe, NM 87504

ISSN 1078-8018
ISBN 1-56261-197-6

Distributed to the book trade by
Publishers Group West
Emeryville, California

Editor Risa Laib
Editorial Support Elizabeth Wolf, Nancy Gillan, Dianna Delling
Production Kathryn Lloyd-Strongin, Sarah Johansson
Maps Dave Hoerlein
Typesetting Marcie Pottern
Cover Design Tony D'Agostino
Design Linda Braun
Printer Banta Company
Interior Cover Photo Leo de Wys/Steve Vidler

Although the author and publisher have made every effort to provide accurate, up-to-date information, they accept no responsibility for loss, injury, bad fish, or inconvenience sustained by any person using this book.

THE BEST DESTINATIONS IN GREAT BRITAIN

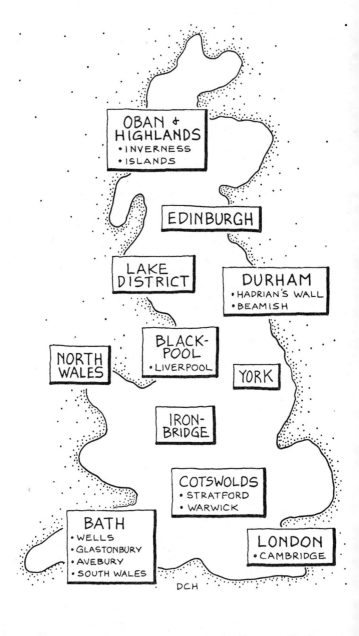

CONTENTS

HOW TO USE THIS BOOK

This book breaks Britain into its top 15 big city, small town, and rural destinations. It then gives you all the information and opinions necessary to wring the maximum value out of your limited time and money in each of these destinations.

If you plan a month or less for England, Scotland, and Wales, and have a normal appetite for information, this lean and mean little book is all you need. If you're a travel info fiend this book sorts through all the superlatives and provides a handy rack upon which to hang your supplemental information.

Experiencing Britain's culture, people, and natural wonders economically and hassle-free has been my goal for 20 years of traveling, tour guiding, and travel writing. With this book, I pass on to you the lessons I've learned, updated for 1995.

Rick Steves' Best of Great Britain is a tour guide in your pocket. Places covered are balanced to include a comfortable mix of exciting big cities and great-to-be-alive-in small towns. It covers the predictable biggies (such as Big Ben, Stratford, Wordsworth's cottage, and bagpipes), while mixing in a healthy dose of Back Door intimacy (nearly edible Cotswold villages, Gaelic folk pubs, angelic boys' choirs, and windswept Roman lookouts). I've been very selective. On a short trip, visiting both Oxford and Cambridge is redundant. I cover just the best—Cambridge. There are plenty of great countryside palaces. I recommend just the best (Blenheim). Sightseeing recommendations are weighted with accessibility in mind.

I don't recommend anything just to fill a hole. If you find no tips on eating in a town, I've yet to find a restaurant worth recommending above the others. In the interest of smart use of your time, I favor accommodations and restaurants handy to your sightseeing activities. Rather than list hotels scattered throughout a city, I describe my favorite two or three neighborhoods, and recommend the best accommodations values in each, from $12 bunk beds to $120 doubles.

The best is, of course, only my opinion. But after two busy decades of travel writing, lecturing, and tour guiding, I've developed a sixth sense of what tickles the traveler's fancy. The places featured in this book will knock your spots off.

This Information Is Accurate and Up-to-Date

This book is updated every year. Most publishers of guidebooks that cover a country from top to bottom can afford an update only every two or three years and even then, it's often by letter. Since this book is selective, covering only Britain's top month of sightseeing, I'm able to personally update it each year. (Don't tell my publisher, but I'm so committed to this book, I'd do it for free.)

Even with an annual update, things change. But if you're traveling with the current edition of this book, I guarantee you're using the most up-to-date information available. If you're packing an old book, you'll learn the seriousness of your mistake by Day Two in England. (Your trip costs about $10 per waking hour. Your time is valuable. This guidebook saves lots of time.)

2 to 22 Days Out . . . Modularity In! Britain's Top Destinations

This book used to be called *2 to 22 Days in Great Britain* and was organized as a proposed 22-day route. It's now restructured into a more flexible modular system. Each recommended module, or "destination," is covered as a mini-vacation on its own, filled with exciting sights; homey, affordable places to stay; and hard opinions on how to best use your limited time. As before, my assumption is that you have limited time and limited money. My goal remains to help you get the most travel experience out of each day and each dollar. Each destination chapter is divided into these sections:

Planning Your Time, a suggested schedule with thoughts on how to best use your time.

Orientation, including transportation within a destination, tourist information, and a map by master mapmaker Dave Hoerlein designed to make the text clear and your entry smooth.

Sights with ratings: ▲▲▲—Don't miss; ▲▲—Try hard to see; ▲—Worthwhile if you can make it; no rating—Worth knowing about.

Sleeping and **Eating**, with addresses and phone numbers of my favorite budget accommodations and restaurants.

   Transportation Connections to nearby destinations
by train and **Route Tips for Drivers** with ideas on roadside
attractions along the way.

   The Appendix is a traveler's toolkit with information on
side-tripping to Ireland, history, architecture, TV for sightseers, climate, telephone numbers, and a British-Yankee
vocabulary list.

   Browse through this book, then choose your favorite
destinations, link them up, and have a great trip. You'll travel
like a temporary local, getting the absolute most out of every
mile, minute, and dollar. You won't waste time on mediocre
sights because, unlike other guidebooks, I cover only my
favorites. Since a major financial pitfall is lousy expensive
accommodations, I've worked hard to assemble the best
accommodations values for each stop. And, as you travel the
route I know and love best, I'm happy you'll be meeting
some of my favorite English, Welsh, and Scottish people.

Costs

Five components make up your trip cost: airfare, surface
transportation, room and board, sightseeing, and
shopping/entertainment/miscellany.

Airfare: Don't try to sort through the mess. Don't go direct.
Find and use a good travel agent. A basic round-trip U.S.A.-
to-London flight costs $500-$1,000, depending on where
you fly from and when. Consider "open-jaws" (e.g., flying
into London and out of Ireland or Scotland).

Surface Transportation: For a three-week whirlwind trip of
all my recommended destinations, allow $450 per person for
public transportation (train pass and key buses), or $500 per
person (based on two people sharing) for a three-week car
rental, tolls, gas, and insurance. Car rental is cheapest if
arranged from the U.S.A. Train passes are normally only
available outside of Europe. You may save money by simply
buying tickets as you go (see below).

Room and Board: You can thrive in Britain on $60 a day
plus transportation costs in 1995. Students and tightwads
will do it on $40. A $50-a-day budget allows $30 for bed and
breakfast, $5 for lunch, and $15 for dinner. That's doable.
But budget sleeping and eating requires the skills and information covered below.

Sightseeing: In big cities, figure $5-$10 per major sight (Imperial War Museum–$5, Edinburgh Castle–$8), $2 for minor ones (climbing church towers), $7 for guided walks and bus tours, $25 for splurge experiences (e.g., Welsh and Scottish folk evenings). An overall average of $15 a day works for most. Don't skimp here. After all, this category directly powers most of the experiences all the other expenses are designed to make possible.

Shopping/Entertainment/Miscellany: This can vary from nearly nothing to a small fortune. Figure $1 per tea, $2 per beer and ice cream cone, $1 per postcard, and $10-$20 for evening entertainment. Good budget travelers find that this category has little to do with assembling a trip full of lifelong and wonderful memories.

Prices, Discounts, and Times

I list prices in pounds (£) throughout the book. To keep things simple, I haven't listed "concessions," which is what the British call discounts. Nearly all places give discounts for seniors (loosely given to anyone retired or willing to call themselves a "senior"), youths (8-18), students, groups of ten or more, and families. Prices, as well as hours, telephone numbers, and so on, are accurate as of late 1994. The economy is flat and inflation is low, so these prices should be pretty accurate in 1995. Britain sticks to its schedule (pronounced "SHED-jool") better than most European countries, but double-check hours and times when you arrive. The hours listed are for peak season. During off-season many places close an hour earlier, and some places are open only on weekends or closed entirely in the winter. Confirm your sightseeing plans locally—especially when traveling between October and May.

You will be tempted to buy the **British Heritage Pass** which gets you into over 500 British Heritage and National Trust properties (£30 for 15 days, £45 for 30 days, sold at airport information desks and the British Travel Centre on Regent Street in London). Of the 500 sights included (a list comes with the pass), here are the sights I describe and recommend for a three-week tour of Britain, along with their adult admission prices. A typical sightseer with three weeks will probably pay to see nearly all of these: Shakespeare's Birthplace and Anne Hathaway's Cottage £5, Blenheim

Palace £7, Caernarfon Castle £4, Caerphilly Castle £2, Culloden Battlefield £2, Edinburgh Castle £5, Georgian House £3, Gladstone's Land £3, Palace of Holyroodhouse £4, Housesteads Roman Fort £2, Roman Baths in Bath £5, Stonehenge £3, Tintern Abbey £2, Tower of London £5, Urquhart Castle £3, Warwick Castle £7, and Wordsworth House £4. Your pass also saves you a £1 on all Guide Friday bus tours (you'll probably take four). This totals £70—and takes the pain out of all these admissions with one big pill.

Whirlwind Three-Week Tour

Britain's Best 22-Day Trip

Day	Plan	Sleep in
1	Arrive in London, bus to Bath	Bath
2	Bath	Bath
3	Pick up car, Avebury, Wells, Glastonbury	Bath
4	South Wales, St. Fagan's, Tintern	Stow/Chipping
5	Explore the Cotswold Villages, Blenheim	Stow/Chipping
6	Stratford, Warwick, Coventry	Ironbridge
7	Ironbridge Gorge museum, Llangollen	Ruthin
8	Highlights of North Wales	Ruthin
9	Liverpool, Blackpool	Blackpool
10	Southern Lakes District	Keswick/farmhouse
11	Northern Lakes District	Keswick/farmhouse
12	Drive north, up west coast of Scotland	Oban
13	Highlights, Loch Ness, Scenic Drive	Highlands/Edinburgh
14	More Highlands or Edinburgh	Edinburgh
15	Edinburgh	Edinburgh
16	Hadrian's Wall, Beamish, Durham	Durham
17	York Moors, York, turn in car	York
18	York	York
19	Early train to London	London
20	London	London
21	London	London
22	Side trip to Cambridge, London	Whew!

Sample Itineraries
Priority of British Sightseeing Stops

3 days:	London
5 days, add:	Bath, Cotswolds, Blenheim
7 days, add:	York
9 days, add:	Edinburgh
11 days, add:	Stratford, Warwick, Cambridge
14 days, add:	North Wales, Wells/Glastonbury/Avebury
17 days, add:	Lakes District, Hadrian's Wall, Durham
21 days, add:	Ironbridge, Blackpool, Scottish Highlands
24 days, add:	South Wales, slow down
30 days, add:	a 5-day swing through Ireland

(The map and suggested 22-day itinerary include everything in the above 24 days.)

Train Travelers: While this 22-day itinerary is designed to be done by car, it can be done by train and bus or, better yet, with a rail 'n' drive pass (best car days: Cotswolds, North Wales, Lakes District, Scottish Highlands, Hadrian's Wall). For three weeks without a car, I'd probably skip the recommended sights with the most frustrating public transportation (South and North Wales, Ironbridge Gorge, the Highlands) and do the Cotswolds with a one-day bus tour. With more time, everything is workable without a car.

Itinerary Tips
Most people fly into London and remain there for a few days. Instead, consider zipping off immediately to a smaller city, such as Bath, and visiting London at the end of your trip. You'll be more rested and ready to tackle Britain's greatest city. Heathrow Airport has direct connections to Bath and other cities.

To give yourself a little rootedness, minimize one-night stands. It's worth a long drive after dinner to be settled into a town for two nights. Besides, B&Bs are quicker to give a good price to someone staying more than one night. Alternate intense and relaxed periods. Every trip (and every traveler) needs at least a few slack days.

Many people save a couple days and a lot of miles by going directly from the Lake District to Edinburgh, skipping the long joyride through Scotland.

I consider Wales, rather than Scotland or Ireland, the best quick look at Celtic Britain. But Ireland is easy to splice in or tack on to the end of your trip.

As you're reading this book, note festivals, colorful market days, and days that sights are closed. Sundays have pros and cons, as they do for travelers in the U.S.A. (special events, limited hours, closed shops and banks, limited public transportation, no rush hours). Saturdays are virtually weekdays. Popular places are even more popular on weekends—especially sunny weekends, which are sufficient cause for an impromptu holiday in the soggy British Isles.

Bank holidays bring most businesses to a grinding halt on Christmas, December 26, New Year's Day, Good Friday, Easter, the first and last Mondays in May, and the last Monday in August.

When to Go

July and August are peak season—my favorite time—with the best weather and the busiest schedule of tourist fun. But peak season is crowded and more expensive than travel in other seasons. This book tackles peak-season problems, especially those of finding a room. Travel during "shoulder season" (May, early June, September, and early October) is easier. Shoulder-season travelers get minimal crowds, decent weather, the full range of sights and tourist fun spots, and the joy of being able to just grab a room almost whenever and wherever they like—often at a flexible price. Winter travelers find absolutely no crowds, soft room prices, but shorter sightseeing hours. The weather can be cold and dreary, and nightfall draws the shades on your sightseeing well before dinnertime.

British weather is reliably unpredictable (but mostly bad), and July and August are not much better than shoulder months. May and June can be lovely. Conditions can change several times in a day, but rarely is the weather extreme. Daily averages throughout the year range between 42 and 70 degrees, and temperatures below 32 or over 80 degrees are cause for headlines. Check the Climate Chart in the Appendix, and carry a jacket or sweater even in July.

Travel Smart

When you arrive in a town, make any necessary arrangements for your departure. Use the telephone for reservations and confirmations, reread this book as you travel, and visit local tourist information offices. Ask questions. Most locals are eager to point you in their idea of the right direction. Carry a phone card, wear a money belt, pack along a pocket-size notebook to organize your thoughts, and practice the virtue of simplicity. Those who expect to travel smart, do.

Consider the travel arrangements and reservations listed below before your trip or within a few days of arrival.

Before You Go
• Reserve a room for your first night.
• If you'll be traveling in July and August, and want to be sure of my lead listings, book the B&Bs on your route (and the Ruthin Medieval Banquet) as soon as you're ready to commit to a date.
• Confirm your car rental and pick-up plans with rental agency.
• If you'll be attending the Edinburgh Festival (August 13-September 2 in 1995), call the festival office at 0131/225-5756 to book a ticket by credit card from April on. And while you're at it, book your Edinburgh room.
• Write to the Tower of London (Yeoman Clerk, Queen's House, Tower of London, London EC3 N4AB) five weeks in advance, with an international reply coupon, requesting an invitation to the moving "Ceremony of the Keys" (the nightly, 21:30, pageantry-filled changing of the keys in the Tower of London, small group of visitors allowed). Say which night or nights you can come (free). While they request five weeks' notice, you might try this with a stamped envelope addressed to your London hotel once you arrive.

Within a Day or Two of Arrival
• If you'll be in London the last night of your trip, reserve a room and book tickets for a London play or concert.
• If the Royal Shakespeare Company will be performing at the Stratford Theater when you're in Stratford, book a ticket (tel. 01789/295623).

Tourist Information (TIs)

Virtually every British town has a helpful tourist information center (TI) eager to make your visit as smooth and enjoyable as possible. Take full advantage of this service. Arrive (or telephone) with a list of questions and a proposed sightseeing plan. Pick up maps, brochures, and walking tour information. Use their room-finding service only as a last resort (bloated prices, fees, no opinions). In London, you can pick up everything you'll need in one stop at the National Tourist Information Centre.

Before your trip, send a postcard to the British Tourist Authority requesting maps, general information, and any specific information you might need (such as a list of upcoming festivals): 551 5th Ave., 7th floor, New York, NY 10176-0799, tel. 212/986-2200, fax 212/786-1188. Their free London and Britain maps are excellent (and the same maps are sold for £1 each at TIs in Britain).

Recommended Guidebooks

This book will help you have an inexpensive, hassle-free trip. *Use this year's edition.* I tell you, you're crazy to save a few bucks by traveling on old information. To rescue those of you who will invariably travel on a two-year-old edition of this book (and realize your mistake too late), I've sent the latest edition of this book to my lead B&Bs in each town for you to transcribe over breakfast.

If you'll be going beyond my recommended destinations or wanting more information on the sights, supplement *Rick Steves' Best of Britain* with a few more guidebooks. I know it hurts to spend $30 or $40 on extra books and maps, but when you consider the money they'll save you and the improvements they'll make in your $3,000 vacation—not buying them would be perfectly penny-wise and £-foolish.

While this book gives you everything you'll need for the structure of your trip, each place you'll stop at has plenty of great little guidebooks to fill you in on the local history. For cultural and sightseeing background in bigger chunks, Michelin and Cadogan guides to London, England, and Britain are good.

Let's Go: Britain and Ireland, written and thoroughly updated annually by Harvard students (new editions come out each January), is a general, low-budget, directory-type guidebook listing a broad range of travel services, accommodations, restaurants, and sights. Get *Let's Go* for information on youth hostels, nightlife, and train travel. It's written for students on low budgets, and even though I'm not a student, I use it every year. *Let's Go* is the best single book for those traveling beyond this book's destinations.

Rick Steves' Books

Rick Steves' Europe Through the Back Door (13th edition, John Muir Publications, 1995) gives you budget-travel skills such as minimizing jet lag, packing light, driving or train travel, finding budget beds without reservations, changing money, theft, terrorism, hurdling the language barrier, health, travel photography, what to do with your bidet, ugly-Americanism, laundry, itinerary strategies, and more. The book also includes chapters on my forty favorite "Back Doors," six of which are in the British Isles.

Rick Steves' Country Guides (Santa Fe, NM: John Muir Publications, 1995) are a series of eight guidebooks covering Europe, France, Italy, Spain/Portugal, Germany/Switzerland/Austria, Scandinavia, and the Baltics/Russia, just as this one covers Britain.

Europe 101: History and Art for the Traveler (co-written with Gene Openshaw, John Muir Publications, 1990) gives you the story of Europe's people, history, and art. A little *101* background knowledge really helps your sightseeing come alive.

Mona Winks (John Muir Publications, 1993, also co-written with Gene Openshaw), gives you fun, easy-to-follow self-guided tours of Europe's top twenty museums. In London, Mona leads the way through the British Museum, the National Gallery, and the Tate Gallery.

My PBS television series, "Travels in Europe with Rick Steves" (13 new shows will air in 1995), includes six half-hour shows on Britain and Ireland. These may re-air on your local station and are now available in information-packed videotapes (see Catalog at the back of this book).

Maps

This book's maps are concise and simple, designed and drawn by Dave Hoerlein. His maps will help you follow my text, locate recommended places, and get you to the tourist office where you'll find a more in-depth map of the city or region (usually free).

Maps to buy in England: Train travelers can do fine with a simple rail map (such as the one that comes with your train pass) and free city maps from the TI as you travel. But drivers shouldn't skimp on maps. If you're driving, get a road atlas (3 miles to 1 inch) covering all of Britain. Ordnance Survey, AA, and Bartholomew editions are available for about £7 in tourist information offices, gas stations, and bookstores. Drivers, hikers, and bikers may want much more detailed maps for the Cotswolds, North Wales, Lake District, and West Scotland.

Transportation in Britain

By Car or Train?
Cars are best for three or more traveling together (especially families with small kids), those packing heavy, and those scouring the countryside. Train and bus are best for single travelers, city-to-city travelers, and blitz tourists.

Britain has a great train-and-bus system, and travelers who don't want to (or can't afford to) drive a rental car can enjoy an excellent tour using public transportation. Britain's 100-mph train system is one of Europe's best. (For a free Britrail map and schedule to plan with, call Britrail in the U.S.A. at 800/677-8585.) Buses go where the trains don't.

My choice is to connect big cities by train and to explore the rural areas (Cotswolds, North Wales, Lake District, and Highlands) footloose and fancy-free by rental car. Consider a BritRail/Drive pass, which gives you various combinations of rail days and car days to use within a month's time.

Deals on Rails, Wheels, Wings
Regular tickets on Britain's great train system (15,000 departures from 2,400 stations daily) are the most expensive per mile in all of Europe. Those who go round-trip, buy in advance, or ride the bus save big. For instance, the regular fare for the 2-hour train trip from York to London is £44 ($70). The APEX fare is only £33 (book 7 days in advance)

BritRail Routes

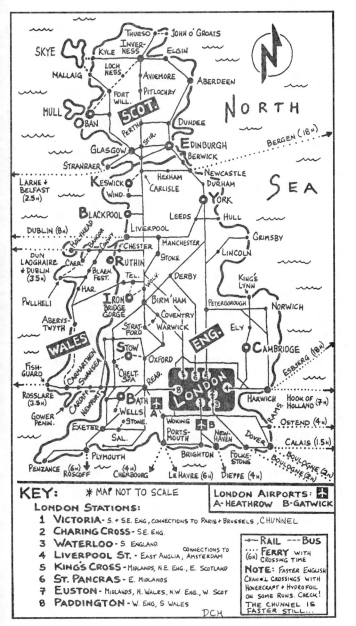

KEY: * MAP NOT TO SCALE

LONDON AIRPORTS: A - HEATHROW B - GATWICK

LONDON STATIONS:
1 **VICTORIA** - S. & S.E. ENG., CONNECTIONS TO PARIS & BRUSSELS, CHUNNEL
2 **CHARING CROSS** - S.E. ENG.
3 **WATERLOO** - S ENGLAND
4 **LIVERPOOL ST.** - EAST ANGLIA, AMSTERDAM CONNECTIONS TO
5 **KING'S CROSS** - MIDLANDS, N.E. ENG., E. SCOTLAND
6 **ST. PANCRAS** - E. MIDLANDS
7 **EUSTON** - MIDLANDS, N. WALES, N.W. ENG., W SCOT
8 **PADDINGTON** - W. ENG, S WALES

•━━• RAIL ---BUS
(6H) •••• FERRY WITH CROSSING TIME
NOTE: FASTER ENGLISH CHANNEL CROSSINGS WITH HOVERCRAFT & HYDROFOIL ON SOME RUNS. CHECK! THE CHUNNEL IS FASTER STILL...

DCH

Cost of Public Transportation

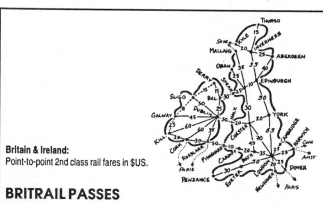

Britain & Ireland:
Point-to-point 2nd class rail fares in $US.

BRITRAIL PASSES

Validity in consec. days	Adult first cl.	Adult standard	over 60 first cl.	over 60 standard	16-25 youth standard
8	$299	$219	$279	$199	$179
15	489	339	455	305	269
22	615	425	555	379	339
1 month	715	495	645	445	395

1994 prices.

BRITRAIL FLEXIPASSES

4 days in 1 month	$249	$189	$229	$169	$155
8 days in 1 month	389	269	350	245	219
15 days in 1 month	575	395	520	355	----
15 days in 2 months	----	----	----	----	309

1994 prices. Overnight journeys begun on your BritRail pass or flexipass's final night can be completed the day after your pass expires—only BritRail allows this trick. British couchettes cost a steep $37.

BRITRAIL DRIVE PASSES

	standard class	first class
Any 3 days by rail + 3 days by car in 1 month:	$280	$330
Any 6 days by rail + 7 days by car in 1 month:	$548	$648

1994 prices. BritRail Drive packages give you rail travel throughout England, Scotland and Wales and use of a Hertz car in Great Britain. Prices listed are per person, with two traveling together for a class B (manual 2-door 4-seat) economy car. Add about $15 for class C and another $15 for class D cars. Drivers must be 21. Seniors over 60 save $20 on these rates. Your travel agent can give you a complete description of this complex program.

and the SuperSaver fare is £45 round-trip (no advance booking necessary, but no travel allowed on Friday or during morning rush hour, open return). The bus makes the trip from York to London in 4 hours for about £35. Round-trip bus tickets usually cost no more than one-way fares.

The pattern is clear and consistent: trains are twice as fast and 50 percent more expensive than buses. But buses go many places that trains don't. Anything is much cheaper if you go round-trip.

Railpasses can be a good deal. The BritRail pass comes in "consecutive day" and "flexi" versions, with price breaks for second class ("standard" class), youths, and seniors. BritRail passes cover England, Scotland, and Wales. There are now Scotland passes, England/Wales passes, and a new BritIreland pass. And there are several "BritRail Drive" passes, which allow you to take a day of rail here and a day of car rental there. These passes are sold outside of Europe only. For specifics, contact your travel agent or Europe Through the Back Door (tel. 206/771-8303).

Budget travelers can save a wad with a bus pass. These are sold in the U.S.A. (800/327-6097) for 20 percent more than the price you'd pay in Britain. The National Express sells the following Tourist Trail bus passes (over the counter): 5 days (£65), 8 days (£90), 15 days (£135), 22 days (£160), and 30 days (£190). Those over age 59 and under 24 save 33 percent. Bus stations are normally at or near train stations. The British distinguish between "buses" (for local runs with lots of stops) and "coaches" (long distance, express runs).

Backpacker's Bus Circuits: There are several super cheap, hop-on-and-hop-off bus circuits that take mostly youth hostelers around the country cheap and easy. For instance, **Slow Coach** does a 1,600 kilometer circle connecting London, Bath, Stratford, the Lakes, Edinburgh, York, Cambridge, and London youth hostels (2-month pass £70, tel. 01249/891959). **Haggis Backpacker** offers a similar deal around Scotland (1,000 km: Edinburgh, Inveraray, Oban, Glencoe, Fort William, Skye, Inverness, Edinburgh, tel. 0131/557-9393) for £55. Anyone is welcome.

British Midland Airline has some reasonable flights: London/Heathrow-Edinburgh (8/day, 75 min, £85 one-way, £74 stand-by), Heathrow-Dublin (10/day, 70 min, £95). If

you've got more money than time, don't buy a long train
ticket without considering a BM flight (tel. 0181/745-7321
or 01345/554554 for 24-hour recorded schedule info).

Car Rental

Car rental for this tour is cheapest if arranged in advance
through your hometown travel agent. To get the best price,
ask for the weekly rate with unlimited mileage and ask about
leasing. You can pick up and drop off just about anywhere,
any time. If you pick up the car in a smaller city, such as
Bath, you'll have an easier time adjusting to driving on the
other side of the road. If you drop it off early or keep it
longer, you'll be credited or charged at a fair, pro-rated
price. Big companies have offices in most cities. (Ask to be
picked up at your hotel.) Small local rental companies (such
as Terminal Car Rental and Alamo Car Rental) can be
cheaper but aren't as flexible.

The Ford 1.3-liter Escort-category car costs about $50
per week more than the smallest cars but feels better on the
motorways and safer on the small roads. For peace of mind, I
spring for the CDW insurance (Collision Damage Waiver,
about $10 per day), which gives a zero-deductible rather
than the standard value-of-the-car "deductible." Remember,
minibuses are a great budget way to go for five to nine
people.

Driving British

Driving in Britain is basically wonderful—once you remember to stay on the left and after you've mastered the "roundabouts." But be warned: every year, I get a few cards from
traveling readers advising me that for them, trying to drive
British was a nerve-wracking and regrettable mistake.
Here are a few tips:

Your U.S.A. license is all you need. A British
Automobile Association membership comes with most
rentals. Understand its towing and emergency road service-
type benefits. Gas (petrol) costs about $3 per gallon and is
self-serve. Know what octane (star) rating your car takes,
push the correct button, and pump away. Seat belts are
required by law. Speed limits are 30 mph in town, 70 mph
on the motorways, and 60 mph elsewhere. The national sign

for 60 mph is a white circle with a black slash. Avoid big cities whenever possible. Most have modern ring roads to skirt the congestion. The shortest distance between any two points is usually the motorway. Road signs can be baffling unless you read them with the help of your map.

Parking is confusing. One yellow line marked on the pavement means no parking Monday through Saturday during work hours. Double yellow lines mean no parking at any time. Broken yellow lines mean short stops are okay, but always look for explicit signs or ask a passing passerby.

Even in small towns, parking in Britain can be a royal headache. Rather than fight it, I just pull into the most central and handy car park I can find; follow the big blue "P" signs. I keep a bag of 10p and 20p coins in the ashtray for parking meters. Copy your car key as soon as possible so you won't get locked out and your partner can enjoy access to the car. Buy some Windex for cleaner sightseeing.

Sleeping in Britain

I've described my recommended hotels and B&Bs with a standard code. The prices are for one-night stays in peak season, include a hearty English breakfast, and assume you're going direct and not through a tourist information office. Prices may be soft for off-season and longer stays. While many places have larger rooms and offer families special deals, Britain is peculiar in its insistence on charging per person rather than per room. Because of this, small groups usually pay the same for a single and a double as they would for a triple.

The Accommodations Description Code

S—Single room, or price for one person in a double.
D—Twin or double room. (I specify double- and twin-bedded rooms only if they are priced differently, or if a place has only one or the other.)
T—Three-person room (often a double bed with a single).
Q—Four-person room (adding an extra child's bed to a T is usually cheaper).
B—*En suite* rooms which, in Britain, have a toilet and a shower (most likely) or bath. All rooms have a sink. Any room without a B has access to a free B on the corridor.

WC—Toilet in the room. Unless I specify some rooms B and some BWC, B rooms normally have a WC.

CC—Accepts credit cards: **V**=Visa, **M**=Mastercard, **A**=American Express. With no CC mention, assume they accept only cash.

No smoking—While most places allow smoking in the sleeping rooms and not in the breakfast room, many are going smoke-free. I'll note these, as well as places that smell musty.

Family deal—Indicates that parents with young children can easily get a room with an extra child's bed or a discount for larger rooms.

Elevator—Almost every place has three floors of rooms, steep stairs, and no elevator. Offhand, I can't think of a single elevator among my recommended places. If you're concerned about stairs, call and ask about ground-floor rooms.

According to this code, a couple staying at a "DB-£30, CC:VM" hotel would pay a total of £30 a night for a room with a toilet and shower (or bath). A "cooked English breakfast" is included. The hotel accepts Visa, Mastercard, or cash. Since no other type of room is mentioned, the hotel has only DBs (*en suite* two-person rooms).

B&Bs in Britain

Thank God Britain has such lousy hotels, because the bed-and-breakfast alternative gives you double the cultural intimacy for half the price.

I'm assuming you have a reasonable but limited budget. Skip hotels. Go the B&B way. If you can use a telephone and speak English, you'll enjoy homey, friendly, clean rooms at a great price by sticking to my listings.

If you're traveling beyond my recommended destinations, you'll find B&Bs where you need them. Any town with tourists has a tourist information office that books rooms or can give you a list and point you in the right direction. In the absence of a TI, ask people on the street for help.

B&Bs range from large guest houses with 15 to 20 rooms to small homes renting out a spare bedroom. The philosophy of the management determines the character of a place more than its size and facilities offered. Avoid places run as a business by absentee owners. My top listings are run by couples who enjoy welcoming the world to their breakfast table. Small places (with a gross income of under £35,000) don't have to pay a 17½ percent tax and offer cheaper prices. Small places can also skimp on safety regulations, allowing them to operate cheaper yet.

You'll pay £12-£28 for a B&B in 1995 ($18-$42 per person). This includes a big cooked breakfast. How much coziness, tea, and biscuits are tossed in varies tremendously.

The B&Bs I've recommended are nearly all stocking-feet comfortable and very "homely," as they say in England. My prerequisites for recommending a place are that it must be: friendly; in a central, safe, quiet neighborhood; clean, with good beds and a sink in the room and shower down the hall; a good value; not mentioned in other guidebooks (therefore, filled mostly by English travelers); and willing to hold a room until 16:00 or so without a deposit (though more and more places are requiring a deposit or credit card number). In certain cases my recommendations don't meet all these prerequisites. I'm more impressed by a handy location and a fun-loving philosophy than a checklist of facilities.

I promised the owners of the places I list that you will be reliable when you make a telephone reservation; please don't let them (or me) down. If you'll be delayed or won't make it, simply call in. Americans are notorious for "standing up" B&Bs. Being late is no problem if you are in telephone contact.

A few tips: B&B proprietors are selective as to whom they invite in for the night. Risky-looking people (two or more single men are often assumed to be troublemakers) find many places suddenly full. If you'll be staying for more than one night you are a "desirable." Sometimes staying several nights earns you a better price—ask about it. If you book through a TI (tourist information office), it'll take a 10 percent commission. If you book direct, the B&B gets it all (and you'll have a better chance of getting a discount). Nearly all B&Bs have plenty of stairs. Expect good exercise and be happy you packed light. If one B&B is full, ask for guidance. (Mentioning this book can help.) Owners usually work together and can call up an ally to land you a bed. "Twin" means two single beds, and "double" means one double bed. If you'll take either one, let them know or you might be needlessly turned away. "Standard" rooms come with just a sink. More and more are going *en suite*, meaning with a private shower/tub and a "loo." Many better places have a basic room (with a shower down the hall) that they don't even advertise. Unlike on the Continent, twin/double, shower/tub does not effect the price.

B&Bs are not hotels. If you want to ruin your relationship with your hostess, treat her like a hotel clerk. Americans often assume they'll get new towels each day. The British don't, and neither will you. Hang them up to dry and reuse.

The British Tourist Board rates hotels and B&Bs with a crown system. B&Bs are rated as follows: no crowns (basic, clean, one bath per 12 people, safe); one crown (no nylon bed linen, a sink in the room, one bath per eight people); two crowns (tea and coffee in room on request, TV in room or lounge, luggage help); three crowns (hot evening meals, one-third of rooms with bathroom); four crowns (three-fourths of rooms with bathroom, nearly a hotel); five crowns (all with private bathroom, valet, porters, virtually a high-class hotel). Some idealistic guest-house proprietors are refusing to bow to the pressure to fill their B&Bs with all the gimmicks and extras. They continue to offer just a good bed with a shower down the hall, a traditional breakfast, and a warm welcome. They go unlisted, but are an excellent value. Too bad that in our "civilized" world, simplicity is subversive.

But there is hope. Realizing that the facilities-based crown system was too impersonal, the tourist board added a rating measuring the cozy, personal, intangible touches (commended, highly commended, deluxe). While I don't worry much about either rating, coziness supersedes crowns.

While it's possible to travel through Britain at any time of year without reservations, it's best to call ahead and nail down rooms in my best listings as soon as you can say when you'll be there and don't mind the commitment. Generally a phone call with a promise to reconfirm a day in advance will hold a room. Long distance is cheap and easy from public phone booths. Many places will ask for a credit-card number or a traveler's check and will send you a map and confirmation letter. Given the high stakes, erratic B&B values, and the quality of the gems I've found for this book, I'd highly recommend calling ahead for rooms (before your trip or a couple days in advance as you travel).

Youth Hostels

Britain has 400 youth hostels of all shapes and sizes. They can be historic castles or depressing huts, serene and comfy or overrun by noisy children. Unfortunately, they have become overpriced and, in general, I no longer recommend them unless (a) you're on a very tight budget and want to cook your own meals, or (b) you're traveling with a group that doesn't have much money and likes to sleep on bunk beds in big rooms. If you're traveling alone, hosteling is the best way to conquer hotel loneliness. Hostels are also a tremendous source of local and budget travel information. If you hostel selectively, you'll enjoy historical and interesting buildings.

You'll pay an average of £8 for a bed, £1 for sheets, and £2 for breakfast. Anyone can hostel in Britain. If you don't have a hostel card, you can get a one-night guest membership for £1.50. If you plan to hostel, use the excellent British hostel guidebook, available at any hostel. Backpacker-type hotels are popping up all over offering less restrictions and an easier-going atmosphere for around £7 a bunk.

Eating in Britain

I don't mind English food. But then, I liked dorm food, too. True, England isn't famous for its cuisine and probably never will be, but we tourists have to eat. If there's any good place to cut corners to stretch your budget in Britain, it's in eating. Here are a few tips on budget eating:

The English (or Scottish or Welsh) "fry" is famous as a hearty way to start the day. Also known as a "heart attack on a plate," the breakfast is especially feasty if you've just come from the land of the skimpy continental breakfast across the Channel. Your standard fry gets off to a healthy start with juice and cereal or porridge. (Try Weetabix, a soggy English cousin of shredded wheat. Scotland serves great porridge.) Next, with tea or coffee, you get a heated plate with a fried egg, lean Canadian-style bacon, a pretty bad sausage, a grilled tomato, and often a slice of delightfully greasy pan toast, baked beans, and sautéed mushrooms. Toast comes on a rack (to cool quickly and crisply) with butter and marmalade. This meal tides many travelers over until dinner. Order only what you'll eat. A B&B hostess, your temporary local mother, doesn't like to see food wasted.

Many B&Bs don't serve breakfast until 8:30. If you need an early start, ask politely if it's possible. Consider skipping breakfast on occasion if a quick start is important.

Picnicking for lunch saves time and money. If you're traveling by car, outfit the back seat with a cardboard-box pantry: boxes of orange juice (pure by the liter), fresh bread, tasty English cheese, meat, a tube of Colman's English mustard, local eatin' apples, bananas, small tomatoes, rice crackers, gorp or nuts, chocolate-covered "Digestive Biscuits," and any local specialties. Toss in a plastic water-bottle, disposable cups, paper towels, ziplock baggies, and a Swiss Army knife. At open-air markets and supermarkets, you can easily get food in small quantities. (Three little tomatoes and two bananas cost me 40p.) Decent sandwiches (£1.50) are sold everywhere. I often munch "meals on wheels" in a car, train, or bus to save 30 precious minutes and enjoy a relaxed meal.

Although British restaurants are fairly expensive, there are plenty of cheap alternatives: fish-and-chips joints, Chinese and Indian take-outs, cafeterias, pubs (see below), B&Bs that serve evening meals, and your typical, good old greasy-spoon cafés. Bakeries have meat pies (and microwaves), pastries, yogurt and cartons of "semi-skimmed" milk—ideal for fresh, fast, cheap lunches.

Pub Grub and Beer

Pubs are a basic part of the British social scene, and whether you're a teetotaler or a beer-guzzler, they should be a part of your travel here. Pub is short for "public house." It's an extended living room where, if you don't mind the stickiness, you can feel the pulse of Britain. Most traditional atmospheric pubs are in the countryside and smaller towns. Unfortunately, many city pubs have been afflicted with an excess of brass, ferns, and video games. In any case, smart travelers use the pubs to eat, drink, get out of the rain, and make new friends.

Pub grub, which is getting better each year, is Britain's best eating value. For £5, you'll get a basic budget hot lunch or dinner in friendly surroundings. The *Good Pub Guide*, published annually by the British Consumers Union, is excellent. I recommend certain pubs, but food can spoil, and your B&B host usually takes pride in being right up to date on the best neighborhood pub grub. Ask for advice.

Pubs generally serve assorted meat pies (such as steak and kidney pie, shepherd's pie), curried dishes, fish, quiche, vegetables, and invariably chips and peas. Servings are hearty, service is quick, and you'll rarely spend more than £4 to £6 ($6-$9). Your beer or cider adds another dollar or two. Free tap water is always available. A "ploughman's lunch" is a modern "traditional English meal" that nearly every tourist tries . . . once. Pubs that advertise their food and are crowded with locals are less likely to be the kind that serve only lousy microwaved snacks.

The British take great pride in their beer. They think that drinking beer cold and carbonated, as Americans do, ruins the taste. At pubs, long "hand pulls" are used to pull the traditional rich-flavored "real ales" up from the cellar. These are the connoisseur's favorites: fermented naturally, varying from sweet to bitter, often with a hoppy or nutty flavor. Notice the fun names. Experiment with the obscure local micro-brews. Short "hand pulls" at the bar mean colder and fizzier mass-produced and less-interesting keg beers. Mild beers are sweeter with a creamy malt flavoring. Stout is dark and more bitter, like Guinness. For a cold, refreshing, basic American-style beer, ask for a "lager." Try the draft cider . . . carefully. English ladies like a half-beer and half-lemonade "shandy." Teetotalers can order a soft drink. Drinks are served by the pint or the half-pint. (It's almost feminine for a man to order just a half; I order mine with quiche.) Don't wait to be served. Jostle right up to the bar and pay as you're served. Tipping is expected only of those who've drunk way too much.

Pub hours vary. The strictly limited wartime hours were finally ended a few years ago, and now pubs can serve beer from 11:00 to 23:00, and Sunday from noon to 22:30. Children are served food and soft drinks in pubs, but you must be 18 to order a beer. People go to a "public house" to be social. They want to talk. Get vocal with a local. Pubs are the next best thing to relatives in every town.

Pounds and Pence

The British pound sterling (£) is broken into 100 pence (p). A pound, or "quid," is worth about $1.50. Pence means "cents." You'll find coins ranging from 1 pence to £1 and bills from

£5 to £50. Multiply British prices by 1.5 to figure pounds into dollars: £6 is $9, £4.50 is about $7, and 80p is $1.20.

Scotland and Ireland have their own currencies. English and Scottish money are worth the same and are good in both countries. The Irish-English money relationship is like the Canadian-American one. English money is a little more valuable. Ireland is a different country—treat it that way.

Britain's 17.5 percent sales tax, the "value added tax" or VAT, is built into nearly everything you buy. Tourists can get a refund of this VAT on souvenirs they take out of the country, but it's often a headache. Unless you buy something worth several hundred dollars, your refund won't be worth the delays, incidental expenses, and headaches that complicate the lives of TISVATR (Tourists in Search of VAT Refunds).

Even in jolly old England you should use traveler's checks and a money belt. Thieves smartly target tourists. I would. A money belt (see Catalog at back of book) is peace of mind. You can carry lots of cash safely in a money belt. (And, given the high bank fees, you should.)

Many traveling exclusively in Great Britain buy traveler's checks in pounds sterling. While policies vary, some British banks favor various traveler's checks by waiving the commission fee (Barclays checks and related "interpayment" checks at Barclays banks, American Express checks at Lloyds banks, Thomas Cook checks at Midland banks or Cook offices). This can save you around 2 percent. But don't let this cloud your assessment of that bank's exchange rates. Save time and money by changing plenty of money at a time (Banks' charges often exceed £4.) On my last trip, I bought all my pounds in cash from a good American foreign exchange service, stowed them safely in my money belt, and never needed a British bank.

Credit cards are not very widely accepted in Britain. I bring a credit card only because it's necessary for renting a car. Spend cash, not plastic, as you travel. If you'll be getting cash advances on your credit card, you'll find that Barclays, National Westminster, and places displaying an Access or Eurocard sign accept Mastercard. Visa is accepted at Barclays and Midland banks.

Red Tape and Business Hours

You currently need a passport but no visa and no shots to travel in Britain. In Britain—and in this book—you'll be using the 24-hour clock. After 12:00 noon, keep going— 13:00, 14:00 . . . For anything over 12, subtract 12 and add p.m. (14:00 is 2:00 p.m.).

This book lists in-season hours for sightseeing attractions. Off season, roughly October through April, expect generally shorter hours, more lunchtime breaks, and fewer activities.

Europeans arrange dates by day/month/year, so Christmas is 25-12-95. What we Americans call the second floor of a building is the first floor in Europe.

Telephoning in Britain

Use the telephone routinely. You can make long-distance calls directly, cheaply, and easily, and there's no language barrier. Call ahead to reserve or reconfirm rooms, check opening hours, confirm tour times, and reserve theater tickets. I call home rather than mess with postcards.

The British telephone system is great. Easy-to-find public phone booths are either coin- or card-operated. Newer phones ingeniously take any coin from 10p to £1, and a display shows how your money supply's doing. Only completely unused coins will be returned, so put in biggies with caution. The new and ever more prevalent telephone card is wonderfully convenient. Buy £2, £4, or £10 phone cards at newsstands, hotels, tourist offices, or post offices and use them for ease and economy. Ignore the Mercury phone booths and stick with the dominant British Telecom system.

The only tricky phones you'll use are the expensive Mickey-Mouse coin-op ones in bars and B&Bs. Some require money before you dial and others only after you've connected. Many have a button you must push before you begin talking. But all have clear instructions. Long distance in Britain is most expensive from 8:00-13:00, cheaper from 13:00-18:00, and cheapest from 18:00-8:00. A short call across the country is quite inexpensive. Don't hesitate to call long-distance.

To call long-distance, you'll need the correct area code. Britain has about as many area codes as we have prefixes. For local calls, just dial the three- to seven-digit number. For long-distance (trunk) calls, you'll find area codes listed by city on phone booth walls, from directory assistance (free and happy to help, dial 142 in London, 192 outside of London), and throughout this book. For a telephone directory, see the Appendix at the back of this book.

In 1995 Britain is changing all its area codes. Local numbers will not change, but every area code will grow one digit with a "1" inserted after the "0." Therefore central London will go from 071 to 0171. Edinburgh will go from 031 to 0131. I have listed the new area codes in this book. If you have old information you can update the area codes yourself.

To call Britain from another country, replace the beginning zero of the area code with the country code. For instance, Britain's country code is 44 and London's area code is 0171. My London B&B's number is 727-7725. To call it from New York, I dial 011 (the U.S.A.'s international code), 44 (Britain's country code), 171 (London's area code without the 0), then 727-7725. To call it from old York, dial 0171/727-7725.

To call my office from Britain, I dial 00 (Britain's international code), 1 (U.S.A.'s country code), 206 (my Seattle area code), and 771-8303. Calling the U.S.A. from Britain usually costs more than double the U.S.A.-to-Britain rate. But if you use a "USA Direct" service, you'll be charged the lower U.S.A.-to-Britain rate, plus a $2.50 service fee. You'll save money on calls of 3 minutes or more. For 20p, you can actually call home for 5 seconds—long enough to say "call me," or to make sure an answering machine is off so you can call back, using your USA Direct card to connect with a person. USA Direct services are offered by Sprint, AT&T, and MCI (listed in Appendix).

Stranger in a Strange Land

We travel all the way to Great Britain to experience something different—to become temporary locals. Americans have a knack for finding certain truths to be God-given and self-evident—such as cold beer; a bottomless coffee cup; long, hot showers; and driving on the right-hand side of the road. One of the beauties of travel is the opportunity to see that there are logical, civil, and even better alternatives. If there is a negative aspect of the British image of you and me, we are big, loud, aggressive, impolite, rich, and a bit naive. The American worker earns twice the salary of his British counterpart, yet taxes, unemployment, and the cost of living are all higher for the British worker.

Still, I find warmth and friendliness throughout Great Britain. An eagerness to go local ensures that I enjoy a full dose of British hospitality.

Europeans, in general, admire and support a strong America. The British like us even though many will remind us that our high-flying national eagle is not perfectly house-trained. While Europeans look bemusedly at some of our Yankee excesses—and worriedly at others—they nearly always afford us individual travelers all the warmth we deserve.

Send Me a Postcard, Drop Me a Line

If you enjoy a successful trip with the help of this book and would like to share your discoveries, please send any tips, recommendations, criticisms, or corrections to me at Europe Through the Back Door, Box 2009, Edmonds, WA 98020. To update the book before your trip or share tips, tap into our free computer bulletin board travel-information service (206/771-1902:1200 or 2400/8/N/1). All correspondents will receive a two-year subscription to our *Back Door Travel* quarterly newsletter (it's free anyway).

Judging from the positive feedback and happy postcards I receive from travelers using this book, it's safe to assume you're on your way to a great British vacation—independent, inexpensive, and with the finesse of an experienced traveler. Thanks, and happy travels!

BACK DOOR TRAVEL PHILOSOPHY
As Taught in *Rick Steves' Europe Through the Back Door*

Travel is intensified living—maximum thrills per minute and one of the last great sources of legal adventure. Travel is freedom. It's recess, and we need it.

Experiencing the real Europe requires catching it by surprise, going casual . . . "Through the Back Door."

Affording travel is a matter of priorities. (Make do with the old car.) You can travel—simple, safe, and comfortable—anywhere in Europe for $50 a day plus transportation costs. In many ways, spending more money only builds a thicker wall between you and what you came to see. Europe is a cultural carnival, and time after time you'll find that its best acts are free and the best seats are the cheap ones.

A tight budget forces you to travel close to the ground, meeting and communicating with the people, not relying on service with a purchased smile. Never sacrifice sleep, nutrition, safety, or cleanliness in the name of budget. Simply enjoy the local-style alternatives to expensive hotels and restaurants.

Extroverts have more fun. If your trip is low on magic moments, kick yourself and make things happen. If you don't enjoy a place, maybe you don't know enough about it. Seek the truth. Recognize tourist traps. Give a culture the benefit of your open mind. See things as different but not better or worse. Any culture has much to share.

Of course, travel—like the world—is a series of hills and valleys. Be fanatically positive and militantly optimistic. If something's not to your liking, change your liking. Travel is addicting. It can make you a happier American, as well as a citizen of the world. Our Earth is home to nearly 6 billion equally important people. It's humbling to travel and find that people don't envy Americans. They like us, but with all due respect, they wouldn't trade passports.

Globe-trotting destroys ethnocentricity. It helps you understand and appreciate different cultures. Travel changes people. It broadens perspectives and teaches new ways to measure quality of life. Many travelers toss aside their hometown blinders. Their prized souvenirs are the strands of different cultures they decide to knit into their own character. The world is a cultural yarn shop. And Back Door Travelers are weaving the ultimate tapestry. Come on, join in!

LONDON

London, more than 600 square miles of urban jungle with 7 million struggling people, many of whom speak English, is a world in itself, a barrage on all the senses. On my first visit, I felt very, very small. London is much more than its museums and famous landmarks. It's a living, breathing organism that manages to thrive.

London has changed dramatically in recent years, and many visitors are surprised to find how "un-English" it is. Whites are now actually a minority in major parts of a city that once symbolized white imperialism. Arabs have nearly bought out the area north of Hyde Park. Chinese take-outs now outnumber fish-and-chips shops (or "fee'n' chee" shops as some locals call them). Many hotels are run by people with foreign accents (who hire English chambermaids), while outlying suburbs are home to huge communities of Indians and Pakistanis. London is learning—sometimes fitfully—to live as a microcosm of its formerly vast empire.

With just a few days here, you'll get no more than a quick splash in this teeming human tidepool. But, with a quick orientation, you'll get a good sampling of its top sights, history, cultural entertainment, and ever-changing human face.

Blow through London on the open deck of a double-decker orientation tour bus, and take a pinch-me-I'm-in-Britain walk through downtown. Ogle the crown jewels at the Tower of London, hear the chimes of Big Ben, and see the Halls of Parliament in action. Hobnob with the tombstones in Westminster Abbey, duck WWII bombs in Churchill's underground Cabinet War Rooms, and brave the earth-shaking Imperial War Museum. Overfeed the pigeons at Trafalgar Square. Visit with Leonardo, Botticelli, and Rembrandt in the National Gallery. Whisper across the dome of St. Paul's Cathedral and rummage through our civilization's attic at the British Museum. Cruise down the Thames River. You'll enjoy some of Europe's best people-watching at Covent Gardens and the Buckingham Palace Changing of the Guard. Just sit in Victoria Station, at a major tube station, at Piccadilly Square, or on Trafalgar Square, and observe. Spend one evening at a theater and the others catching your breath.

Planning Your Time:
Three Days in London

The sights of London alone could easily fill a trip to Britain. But on a three-week tour of Britain, I'd give it three busy days. If you're flying in, consider starting your trip in Bath and letting London be your British finale. Especially if you hope to enjoy a play or concert, a night or two of jet lag is bad news. Here's a suggested three-day schedule:

Day 1:

 9:00   Tower of London (Beefeater tour, crown jewels).

12:00   Picnic on Thames, cruising from Tower to Westminster Bridge.

13:00   Big Ben, Halls of Parliament, Westminster Abbey, walk up Whitehall, visit the Cabinet War Rooms.

16:00   Trafalgar Square, National Gallery.

17:30   Visit National Tourist Information Centre near Piccadilly, planning ahead for your trip.

18:30   Dinner near Piccadilly. Take in a play?

Day 2:

 9:00   Spend 30 minutes in a phone booth getting all essential elements of your trip nailed down. If you know where you'll be and when, call those B&Bs now!

10:00   Take the Round London bus tour. (Consider hopping off for the 11:30 Changing of the Guard at Buckingham Palace.)

12:30   Covent Gardens for lunch and people-watching.

14:00   Tour British Museum.

17:30   Visitor's Gallery in Houses of Parliament (if in session).

19:00   Take in a play, concert, or evening walking tour (if still awake).

Day 3:

 9:00   Choose among these activities for the day: some serious shopping at Harrods or open-air markets, Museum of the Moving Image, Imperial War museum, Tate Gallery, cruise to Greenwich or Kew, tour St. Paul's Cathedral, Museum of London, a walking tour, or an early train to Bath.

18:15   Train to Bath.

19:30   Check into Bath B&B.

After considering nearly all of London's tourist sights, I have pruned them down to just the most important (or fun) for a first visit. You won't be able to see all of these, so don't try. You'll keep coming back to London. After 15 visits myself, I still enjoy a healthy list of excuses to return.

Orientation
(downtown tel. code: 0171, suburban: 0181)
To grasp London comfortably, see it as the old town without the modern, congested sprawl. Most of the visitors' London lies between the Tower of London and Hyde Park—about a 3-mile walk.

Tourist Information
London Tourist Information Centres are located at Heathrow Airport (daily 8:30-18:00, most convenient and least crowded), at Victoria Station (daily 8:00-18:00, shorter hours in winter), at Selfridges Department Store on Oxford Street (regular store hours). The handier National Tourist Info Centre (described below) covers London just about as well as the LTICs. Bring your itinerary and a checklist of questions. Buy a ticket to a play, save a pound by buying your orientation bus tour ticket here, and pick up these publications: *London Planner*, walking tour brochures, theater guide, *Quick Guide to London*, a Britain map (£1), and a London map (£1). The £1 London map is as good as the £4 maps sold in newsstands and well worth while (free from BTA in the U.S.A: 551 5th Ave., #701, New York, NY 10176). Smelling a new source of profit, London TIs are pushing a 50p-per-minute telephone information service. Avoid it.

The National Tourist Information Centre is energetic and impressive (9:00-18:30, Saturday and Sunday 10:00-16:00, a block downhill from Piccadilly Circus at 12 Regent St.). Check out the well-equipped London/England desk, Wales desk (tel. 409-0969), and Ireland desk (tel. 839-8416). At the center's extensive book shop, gather whatever books, maps, and information you'll need for your entire trip. Consider getting the *Michelin Green Guide to Britain* (£7.50). Train travelers can pick up *Let's Go: Britain and Ireland* (£15, 50% over U.S. price) and hostelers may want the *Youth Hostel Association 1995 Guide* (£6). To cover the highlights in this book, consider the following maps: Cotswolds Wyedean Official Tourist Map (£2.60, Tintern to Coventry); the Lake District Touring Map (£3, entire region or just the NW corner, Ordnance Survey); the Wales Tourist Map (£1.50); and the Leisure Touring Map of Scotland (£3.25). Drivers will need a Britain Road Atlas (£7, AA). Stock up. You're your own guide. Be a good one.

The center has a British Rail information desk and an American Express Bank (no change fee, decent rates, Sundays, too). The Scottish Tourist Centre is a block away (19 Cockspur St., tel. 930-8661).

Trains and Buses

London, a major transportation hub in Britain, has a different train station for each region. For schedule information, call the appropriate station. King's Cross covers northeast England and Scotland (tel. 278-2477). Paddington covers west and southwest England and south Wales (tel. 262-6767). For the others, call 928-5100. Buses are considerably cheaper than trains. Give the National Express bus company a call (tel. 730-0202).

Getting Around London

London's taxis, buses, and subway system make a private car unnecessary. In a city this size, you must get comfortable with its public transportation. Don't be timid.

By Taxi: Big, black, carefully regulated cabs are everywhere. I never met a crabby cabbie in London. They love to talk and know every nook and cranny in town. Rides start at £1 and cost about £1 per tube stop. Often legitimate charges are added on, but for a short ride, three people in a cab travel at tube prices. If a cab's top light is on, just wave it down. If that doesn't work, ask for directions to a nearby taxi stand. Telephoning is unnecessary; taxis are everywhere. Stick with the metered cabs.

By Bus: London's extensive bus system is easy to follow if you have a map listing the routes. Get a free map from a TI or tube station. Signs at stops list routes clearly. Conductors are terse but helpful. Ask to be reminded when it's your stop. Just hop on, tell the driver where you're going, pay what he says, grab a ticket, take a seat, and relax. (Go upstairs for the best view.) Buses and taxis are miserable during rush hours, 8:00-10:00 and 16:00-19:00. Rides start at 90p. Get in the habit of hopping buses for quick little straight shots if you have a transit pass.

By Tube: London's subway is one of this planet's great people-movers. Every city map includes a tube map. Rip one out and keep it in your shirt pocket. Navigate by color-coded lines and north (always up on London maps), south, east, or west. (In fact, think in terms of N, S, E, and W in your general London navigation.) Buy your ticket at the window or from coin-op machines to avoid the line (practice a few fares on the punchboard to see how the system works), then descend to the platform level. You'll need your ticket to leave the system. Many tracks are shared by several lines, and electronic signboards announce which train is next. Each train has its final destination or line name above its windshield. Read the system notices clearly posted on the platforms; they explain the tube's latest flood, construction, or bomb scare. Ask questions of locals and watch your wallet. Bring something to do to pass the waits productively, especially on the notoriously tardy Circle Line. When leaving the tube, save time by choosing the best street exit (look at the maps on the walls). "Tubing" is the fastest long-distance transport in town. Any ride in the Central Zone (on or within the Circle Line, including virtually all my recommended sights and hotels) costs 90p. Remember, "subway" means pedestrian underpass in "English." For tube and bus information, call 222-1234.

London Tube and Bus Passes: There are three handy tube/bus passes to consider: The "Travel Card," covering Zones 1 and 2, gives you unlimited travel for a day starting after 9:30 for £2.80. The "LT Card" offers the same benefits, without the "off peak" restriction, for £4. The "7 Day Travel Card" costs £10.50, covers Zone 1, and requires a passport-type photo (cut one out of any old snapshot and bring it from home). All passes are purchased as easily as a normal ticket from any station, and cover both tube and bus transportation. If you figure you'll take three rides, get the day pass.

Helpful Hints

Theft Alert: Be on guard here more than anywhere in Britain for pickpockets and thieves, particularly on public

London, the Underground

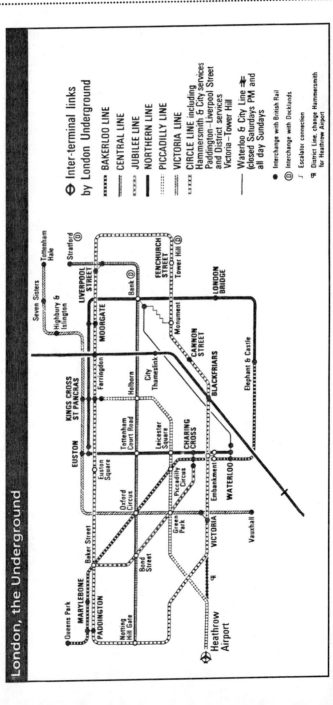

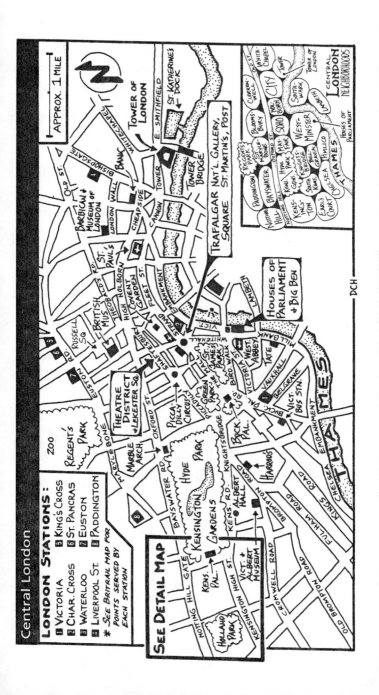

Central London

LONDON STATIONS:
1. VICTORIA 5. KING'S CROSS
2. CHAR. CROSS 6. ST. PANCRAS
3. WATERLOO 7. EUSTON
4. LIVERPOOL ST. 8. PADDINGTON
* SEE BRITRAIL MAP FOR POINTS SERVED BY EACH STATION

SEE DETAIL MAP

CENTRAL LONDON NEIGHBORHOODS

transportation and in places crowded with tourists. Tourists, considered naive and rich, are targeted.

Telephones: In London, dial 999 for emergency help and 142 for directory assistance (both calls are free). The area code for any downtown London phone number is 0171, for suburban London, 0181. Beware of the many area-code-0839 toll numbers. At a TI or post office, buy a handy phone card.

What's Up: For the best listing of what's happening (plays, movies, restaurants, concerts, exhibitions, protests, walking tours, and children's activities), pick up a current copy of *What's On* or *Time Out* (40p more, more theater reviews, more hip) at any newsstand. Call 222-8070 for a taped run-down on "Children's London" (Monday-Friday 16:00-18:00).

Sunday Activities: Few London sights are open on Sunday before 14:00. (Major museums are usually open Sunday afternoons.) Some Sunday morning activities: a church service at St. Paul's, Westminster Abbey, or the Tower of London chapel; Original London Sightseeing Tour by bus; a Thames cruise; Cabinet War Rooms; Imperial War Museum; Museum of the Moving Image; Kew Gardens and Palace; Madame Tussaud's; open-air markets at Petticoat Lane and Campden Market; the Victoria and Albert Museum. Speakers' Corner in Hyde Park gets going at noon.

Sights—London

Hello London Walk—Catch a bus to Westminster Bridge (#12 from Notting Hill Gate or #211 from Victoria Station). Sit on the top deck and relax until the first stop after the bridge. Walk downstream along the Jubilee Promenade for a capital view, then for that "Wow, I'm really in London!" feeling, cross the bridge for a close-up view of the Houses of Parliament and Big Ben (floodlit at night). If you ride the tube (and not the bus), the Westminster stop is right at Big Ben. Walk halfway across the bridge for the great view.

To thrill your loved ones (or bug the envious), call home from a pay phone near Big Ben at about 3 minutes before the hour. (You'll find a phone on Great George Street, across from Parliament Square.) As Big Ben chimes, stick the receiver outside the booth and prove you're in London: Ding dong ding dong . . . dong ding ding dong.

Then cross Whitehall to see the Churchill Statue in the park. (He's electrified to avoid the pigeon problem that stains so many other great statues.) Walk up Whitehall toward Trafalgar Square. Stop at the barricaded and guarded little Downing Street to see #10, home of the British prime minister. Break the bobby's boredom—ask him a question. Just before Trafalgar Square, drop into the Clarence Pub for a reasonable meal or pint of whatever you fancy (cheaper cafeterias and eateries are on the same block or under St. Martin's church on Trafalgar). From Trafalgar, walk to thriving Leicester Square and continue to Piccadilly.

For seediness, walk through Soho (north of Shaftesbury Avenue) up to Oxford Street. From Piccadilly or Oxford Circus you can taxi, bus, or tube home.

▲▲**Original London Sightseeing Tour**—This 90-minute, once-over-lightly, double-decker bus tour drives by all the most famous sights. It comes with a great commentary and provides a stressless way to get your bearings and at least see the biggies. Since you can also "hop on and hop off" at any of the 23 stops and catch a later bus, it's an inexpensive form of transport as well as an informative tour (£10, £9 if you pre-purchase at tourist information offices, daily departures from 9:30 until early evening from Marble Arch, Piccadilly Circus, and Victoria Street, 1 block in front of Victoria Station, reservations unnecessary, ticket good for all the next day if purchased after 14:00, tel. 828-7395.) While every bus leaving from Victoria has a live guide, only every other bus from the other points does. A live guide is worth waiting for. Bring a sweater and extra film. Pick up the wonderful free city map as you board. Note: if you pick up the bus at Victoria (no later than 10:00), you can hop off near the end of the 90-minute loop, a 5-minute walk from Buckingham Palace to catch the changing of the guard. There are several "original" copy-cat tours.

▲▲**Walking Tours**—Several times every day, top-notch local guides lead small groups through specific slices of London's past. While the TI and many hotels have the various flyers, only *Time Out* and *What's On* list all scheduled walks, enabling you to choose according to your schedule and interests. Simply show up at the announced location, pay £4, and enjoy two hours of Dickens, the Plague, Shakespeare,

Legal London, the Beatles, Jack the Ripper, or whatever is on the agenda. Evenings feature organized pub crawls and ghost walks. "London Walks" is the dominant company (for recorded schedule of today's walks, tel. 624-3978).

▲▲**Westminster Abbey** is a crowded collection of England's most famous tombs. Like a stony refugee camp waiting outside St. Peter's gates, this English hall of fame is historic, thought-provoking but a bit over-rated (£4, Monday-Friday 9:00-16:45, Saturday 9:00-14:45 and 15:45-17:45, tel. 222-5152, "super tours" £7, 6/day, 90 min, tel. 222-7110 to book and get times).

▲▲**The Houses of Parliament** (Commons and Lords) are too tempting to terrorists to be opened wide to tourists. But if Parliament is in session, you can view debates in either house at times when most of the building is closed. A light atop Big Ben or a flag flying from the highest tower indicates that Parliament is sitting. (Monday-Thursday 17:15-22:00—long waits until 18:00, Friday 9:30-15:00; use St. Stephens entrance, tel. 219-4272, cloakroom.) The House of Lords has more pageantry, shorter lines, shorter hours, and less-interesting debates (tel. 219-3107). Notice the magnificent hammer-beamed Westminster Hall on the left as you go through security. For the classic view, walk halfway over Westminster Bridge. You won't actually see Big Ben, the 13-ton bell inside the neo-Gothic tower, but you'll hear him. Remember, these old-looking buildings are neo-Gothic—just 19th century, reflecting the Victorian move away from Neoclassicism to a more Christian, medieval style.

▲**Whitehall**, the center-of-government boulevard, runs from Big Ben to Trafalgar past lots of important but mostly boring buildings. Stop by the barricade at #10 Downing Street (the British "White House") and the Horse Guards farther up the street (10:00 -16:00, 11:00 inspection, 16:00 colorful dismounting ceremony, the rest of the day is terrible for camcorders).

▲▲**Cabinet War Rooms**—This is a fascinating walk through the underground headquarters of the British government's fight against the Nazis in the darkest days of the Battle for Britain. Churchill's room, the map room, and so on, are still just as they were in 1945 (£4, daily 10:00-18:00, follow signs, on King Charles St., just off Whitehall).

▲**The Banqueting Hall**, England's first Renaissance building (designed by Inigo Jones in 1625) and one of the few
London landmarks to survive the 1666 fire, is notable for its
Rubens ceiling which, at Charles I's request, drove home the
doctrine of the legitimacy of the divine right of kings. In
1649, divine right ignored, Charles I was beheaded on the
balcony of this building by a Cromwellian parliament.
Admission includes a fine 20-minute audiovisual history, an
interesting-only-to-history-buffs 35-minute tape-recorded
tour, and a look at a fancy banqueting hall (£3, Monday-
Saturday 10:00-17:00, aristocratic WC, immediately across
Whitehall from the Horse Guards, tel. 930-4179).

▲▲**Trafalgar Square**—London's central square is a
thrilling place to just hang out. There's Lord Nelson's towering column surrounded by giant lions (part of the memorial is made from the melted-down cannons of his victims at
Trafalgar), hordes of people, and even more pigeons. (When
bombed, resist the impulse to wipe immediately—it'll smear.
Wait for it to dry and flake off gently.) The square is the
climax of most marches and demonstrations.

▲▲**National Gallery**—Newly renovated, displaying
Britain's top collection of European paintings from 1300 to
1900—works by Leonardo, Botticelli, Velazquez, Rembrandt,
Turner, van Gogh, and the Impressionists—this is one of
Europe's classiest galleries. Don't miss the "Micro Gallery,"
a computer room even your dad could have fun in. You can
study any artist, style, or topic in the museum and even print
out a tailor-made tour map. (Free, Monday-Saturday 10:00-
18:00, Sunday 14:00-18:00, on Trafalgar Square. Tube:
Charing Cross or Leicester Square, free 1-hour tours weekdays at 11:30 and 14:30, Saturdays at 14:00 and 15:30, tel.
839-3321). **The National Portrait Gallery**, just around the
corner, is as exciting as somebody else's yearbook (free, same
hours, tel. 306-0055).

▲▲**Piccadilly**—London's touristy "Town Square" is surrounded by fascinating streets and swimming with youth on
the rampage. Nearby Shaftesbury Avenue and Leicester
Square teem with fun-seekers, theaters, Chinese restaurants,
and street singers. The shiny new Trocadero Center
(between Coventry and Shaftesbury, just off Piccadilly) has
the Guinness World Records Exhibit. Next door, the new

Rock Circus offers a very commercial but serious history of rock music with Madame Tussaud wax stars. It's an entertaining hour under radio earphones for rock 'n' roll romantics (£7, plenty of photo ops, 11:00-22:00).

Soho, to the north of Piccadilly, isn't as sleazy as it used to be, but it's still worth a gawk. This is London's red-light district where "friendly models" wait in tiny rooms up dreary stairways and scantily-clad con artists sell strip shows. Anyone who goes into any one of these shows will be ripped off. Every time. Even a £3 show comes with a £100 cover or minimum (as it's printed on the drink menu). If you object the security man will be called in. The door has no handle until you pay.

▲**Covent Gardens** is a boutique-ish people-watcher's delight with cigarette-eaters, Punch 'n' Judy acts, food that's good for you (but not your wallet), trendy crafts, whiffs of pot, and two-tone (neither natural) hair. For the best lunch deals, walk a block or two away from the eye of this touristic tornado. It's hard to go wrong in a little tea-and-sandwich deli.

▲▲▲**British Museum**—The greatest chronicle of our civilization anywhere, visiting this immense museum is like hiking through Encyclopedia Britannica National Park. After an overview ramble, cover just two or three sections of your choice more thoroughly. The Egyptian, Mesopotamian, Greek (Parthenon), and Manuscripts (Magna Carta, Bibles, Beethoven, and the Beatles) sections are a few of my favorites. (Free, Monday-Saturday 10:00-17:00, Sunday 14:30-18:00, least crowded weekday mornings, tube: Tottenham Court Road, tel. 636-1555.)

▲**Buckingham Palace**—In order to pay for the restoration of fire-damaged Windsor Palace, the royal family is opening their lavish home to the public for the next five summers (£8; August and September only; daily 9:30-17:30; limited to 8,000 a day; come early to get an appointed visit time; tel. 930-5526; if the Queen's not home, leave a message). If the flag is flying, the Queen is home.

▲**Changing of the Guard at Buckingham Palace**—Overrated but almost required. The changing of the guard (most days in summer at 11:30, every other day September-March, no band when wet) is a mob scene. Join the mob at the back side of the palace (the front faces a huge and very private park). The pageantry and parading are colorful and even stirring, but the actual changing of the guard is a non-event. It is interesting to see nearly every tourist in London gathered in one place at the same time. Hop into a big black taxi and say, "To Buckingham Palace, please." For all the color with none of the crowds, see the Inspection of the Guard Ceremony at 11:00 in front of the Wellington Barracks, east of the Palace on Birdcage Walk. Afterwards, stroll through nearby St. James Park.

▲**Hyde Park**—London's "Central Park" has more than 600 acres of lush greenery, a huge man-made lake, a royal palace, and the ornate neo-Gothic Albert Memorial across from the Royal Albert Hall. On Sunday early afternoons, check out Speaker's Corner (tube: Marble Arch). This is soapbox oratory at its best. "The grass roots of democracy" actually is a holdover from when the gallows stood here and the criminal was allowed to say just about anything he wanted to before he swung. I dare you to raise your voice and gather a crowd—it's easy to do.

▲▲**The City of London**—When Londoners say "the City," they mean the 1-square-mile business, banking, and journalism center that 2,000 years ago was Roman Londinium. The outline of the Roman city walls can still be seen in the arc of roads from Blackfriars Bridge to Tower Bridge. Within the City are 24 churches designed by Christopher Wren. It's a fascinating district to wander, but since nobody actually lives there, avoid Saturday and Sunday when it's quiet and empty. Also worth a look is the **Central Criminal Courts**, known as "Old Bailey." An hour in the visitors' gallery is always interesting (at Old Bailey and Newgate St.; Monday-Friday 10:00 -13:00 and 14:00-16:00; quiet in August; tel. 248-3277; no cameras, bags, or cloakroom).

▲▲**St. Paul's Cathedral**—Wren's most famous church is the great St. Paul's, its elaborate interior capped by a 365-foot dome. St. Paul's was Britain's World War II symbol of resistance, as Nazi bombs failed to blow it up. (There's a memorial chapel to the heroic firefighters who kept watch over it with hoses cocked.) The crypt (free with admission) is a world of historic bones and memorials, including Admiral Nelson's tomb. It also has interesting Cathedral models and a worthwhile 15-minute audiovisual story of the church (constant, free). This was the wedding church of Prince Charles and Lady Di. Climb the dome for a great city view and some fun in the whispering gallery. Talk discreetly into the wall and your partner on the far side can hear you. (£3 entry, free on Sunday but restricted viewing due to services, open daily 9:30-16:30, £2.50 to climb the dome, allow an hour to go up and down—good exercise, 90-minute £3 cathedral and crypt tours at 11:00, 11:30, 13:30 and 14:00, tube: St. Paul's, tel. 248-2705.) The **Sir Christopher Wren Pub** (not restaurant) serves good, inexpensive lunches in fun surroundings, just north of the church on Paternoster Square, 11:30-15:00, Monday-Friday.

▲**Museum of London** offers a guided walk through London history—from pre-Roman times to the Blitz (£3, free after 16:30, 10:00-18:00, Sunday 12:00-18:00, closed Monday, tube: Barbican or St. Paul's, tel. 600-3699). This regular stop for the local schoolkids gives the best overview of London history in town.

▲▲▲**Tower of London**—You'll find more bloody history per square inch here than anywhere in Britain. Don't miss the entertaining 50-minute Beefeater tour (free, leaving regularly from inside the gate, last one usually at 15:30) of this historic fortress, palace, prison, and host to more than 3 million visitors a year. Britain's best armory and most lovely Norman chapel are in the White Tower. The crown jewels are the best on earth—and consequently have long midday lines for viewing in July and August. To avoid the crowds, arrive at 9:00 and go straight to the jewels, doing the tour and tower later. (£8, tower hours: Monday-Saturday 9:00-18:30, last entry 17:00, Sunday 10:00-18:30. The long, but fast-moving, line is worst on Sundays. Tube: Tower Hill, tel. 709-0765.) Visitors are welcome on the grounds to worship in the Royal Chapel on Sunday (9:15 communion, 11:00 service with fine choral music, free).

Sights Next to the Tower—The best remaining bit of London's **Roman Wall** is just north of the tower (at the Tower Hill tube station). The **Tower Hill Pageant**, a 15-minute high-tech historical amusement ride takes you through twenty centuries of London history, followed by a small but fine exhibition of Roman and Saxon artifacts uncovered during the recent riverside development. It's worthwhile for rich kids with time to kill (£5.50, daily 9:30-17:30, until 16:30 off-season, across the street from the Tower turnstile, tel. 709-0081). Freshly painted and restored, **Tower Bridge** has an 1894–1994 history exhibit (£5, good view, poor value, daily 10:00-18:30, tel. 403-3761). **St. Katherine Yacht Harbor**, chic and newly renovated, just east of the Tower Bridge, has mod shops and the classic old Dickens Inn, fun for a drink or pub lunch.

▲▲**Cruise the Thames**—Boat tours with an entertaining commentary sail regularly between Westminster Bridge and the Tower (£3.50, round-trip £5, 10:20-17:00, 30 minutes, 3 tours hourly, tel. 930-8589). Leaving from Westminster pier, similar boats also go to Greenwich (£5.60 round-trip, 2 hourly) and Kew Gardens (£7 round-trip, 3/day, 90 min round-trip, tel. 930-2062).

▲▲**Greenwich**—Salty sightseers should make time for England's maritime capital, Greenwich. You can crawl through the *Cutty Sark* (clipper-ship queen of the seas in her day, £3.50), marvel at the little *Gipsy Moth IV* (the 53-foot sailboat Sir Francis Chichester used for his solo voyage around the world in 1967), straddle the zero meridian and set your wristwatch to Greenwich mean time at the Old Royal Observatory, and relive four centuries of Britannia-rules-the-waves history by visiting the National Maritime Museum (£4, 10:00-18:00, Sundays 14:00-18:00, off-season until 17:00, tel. 0181/858-4422). Getting there is either a snap (tube to Island Gardens in Zone 2, free with tube pass, then walk under pedestrian Thames tunnel) or a joy (cruise down the Thames from central London).

▲▲**Tate Gallery**—One of Europe's great houses of art, the Tate specializes in British painting (14th century through contemporary), pre-Raphaelites, Impressionism, and modern art (Matisse, van Gogh, Monet, Picasso). Learn about the mystical watercolorist Blake and the romantic nature-worship art of Turner (free, Monday-Saturday 10:00-18:00, Sunday 14:00-18:00, tube: Pimlico, excellent free tours daily, call for schedule, tel. 887-8000).

▲**Victoria and Albert Museum**—A gangly but surprisingly interesting collection of costumes, armor, furniture, decorative arts, and much more from Asia, Islam, and mostly the

West. Walk through centuries of aristocratic living rooms and follow the evolution of fashion in England (through 40 fascinating and well-described display cases) from 1600 to today (£5 donation politely requested but not required, daily 10:00-18:00, Monday 12:00-18:00, tube: So. Kensington, pleasant garden cafe, tel. 938-8500.)

▲▲**Imperial War Museum**—This impressive museum covers the wars of this century from heavy weaponry to love notes and Varga Girls to Monty's Africa campaign tank to Schwartzkopf's Desert Storm uniform. You can trace the development of the machine gun, watch footage of the first tank battles, hold your breath through the gruesome WWI trench experience, and buy WWII-era toys in the fun museum shop. Rather than glorify war, the museum does its best to shine a light on the powerful human side of one of mankind's most persistent traits. (£3.70, daily 10:00-18:00, free after 16:30, 90 minutes is enough time for most visitors, tube: Lambeth North, tel. 416-5000.)

▲▲**Museum of the Moving Image**—This high-tech, inter-active, hands-on museum traces the story of moving images from a caveman's flickering fire to modern TV. There's great footage of the earliest movies and TV shows. Turn-of-the-century-clad staff speak as if silent films are the latest marvel. You can make your own animated cartoon. Don't miss the speedy 50-year montage of magic MGM moments. (£5.50, daily 10:00-18:00, tube: Embankment, then walk across the Thames pedestrian bridge.)

Honorable Mention—The **Thames Barrier**, the world's largest movable flood barrier, welcomes visitors with an informative and entertaining exhibition (by tube or boat, £2.50, daily 10:00-17:00, tel. 0181/854-1373). At the **Geffrye Decorative Arts Museum** you can walk through British front rooms from 1600 to 1960 (tel. 739-9893). Architects love the quirky **Sir John Soane's Museum** (free). For a fine park and a palatial greenhouse jungle to swing through, take the tube or the boat to **Kew Gardens** (£4, daily 9:30-18:30, Sunday until 20:00, tel. 0181/940-1171).

Day-Trips—You could fill a book with the many easy and exciting day-trips from London (*Daytrips in Britain by Rail, Bus or Car from London and Edinburgh* by Earl Steinbicker, Hastings House). Several tour companies take London-based travelers out and back every day (call Evan Evans at 930-2377 or National Express at 730-0202 for ideas). Evan Evans has three tours which can be used by those without a car as a "free" way to get to Bath or Stow-on-the-Wold (saving you, for instance, the £27 London-Bath train ticket). Tours leave from behind Victoria Station at 9:00 (with your bag stowed under the bus), include a full day of sightseeing with £5 to £10 worth of admissions, and leave you in Bath or Stow before returning to London (£27 Stonehenge and Bath, £42 Salisbury, Stonehenge, Bath, and £39 Oxford, Blenheim, Burford, Stow). The British rail system uses London as a hub and normally offers round-trip fares (after 9:30) that cost the same as one-way fares (e.g., Cambridge, £13.70 normal fare, is £12.30 "cheap day return."). See BritRail's handy "Day Trips from London" booklet. But given the high cost of big-city living and the charm of small-town England, I wouldn't do much day-tripping.

Shopping in London

▲Harrods—One of the few stores in the world that manages to be both big and classy, Harrods is filled with wonderful displays, elegant high teas, and fingernail-ripping riots during its July sales. Harrods has everything from elephants to toothbrushes. Need some peanut butter? The food halls are sights to savor (with reasonable cafeterias, tel. 730-1234). For royal window-shopping, cruise nearby King's Road in Chelsea. Most stores close around 18:00, but stay open until 20:00 on Thursdays.

Street Markets—If you like garage sales and people-watching, hit a London street market. The tourist office has a complete, up-to-date list. Some of the best are: **Berwick Street** (Monday-Saturday 9:00-17:00, produce, tube: Piccadilly), **Jubilee Market** (daily 9:00-17:00, antiques and bric-a-brac on Monday, general miscellany Tuesday-Friday, crafts Saturday-Sunday, tube: Covent Garden), **Kensington Market** (Monday-Saturday 10:00-18:00, a collection of shops with modern and far-out clothing, tube: High Street Kensington), **Petticoat Lane** (Sunday 9:00-13:30, the largest, specializing in general junk, on Middlesex St., tube: Liverpool St.), **Portobello Road** (Saturday 6:00-17:00, flea market, near recommended B&Bs, tube: Notting Hill Gate),

Camden Market (Saturday and Sunday 9:00-17:00; a big, trendy flea market; tube: Camden Town), and **Camden Passage** (Wednesday, Thursday, and Saturday 8:00-15:00, offers a pleasant stroll through lots of expensive antiques on Islington High St., tube: Angel). Warning: street markets attract two kinds of people—tourists and pickpockets.

Famous Auction?—London's famous auctioneers welcome the curious public. For schedules (most weekdays, closed mid-summer), telephone Sotheby's (493-8080, tube: Oxford Circus) or Christie's (839-9060, tube: Green Park).

Entertainment and Theater in London

London bubbles with top-notch entertainment seven nights a week. Everything's listed in the monthly *Time Out* or *What's On* magazines, available at most newsstands. You'll choose from classical, jazz, rock, and far-out music, Gilbert and Sullivan, dance, comedy, Bahai meetings, poetry readings, spectator sports, film, and theater.

London's theater rivals Broadway's in quality and beats it in price. Choose from the Royal Shakespeare Company, top musicals, comedy, thrillers, sex farces, and more. Performances are nightly except Sunday, usually with one matinee a week. Matinees (listed in a box in *What's On*) are cheaper and rarely sold out. Tickets range from about £8 to £25.

Most theaters, marked on tourist maps, are in the Piccadilly-Trafalgar area. Box offices, hotels, and TIs have a handy "Theater Guide" brochure listing everything in town.

The best and cheapest way to book a ticket is simply to call the theater box office directly, ask about seats and dates available, and book by credit card. You can call from the U.S.A. as easily as from England (photocopy your hometown library's London newspaper theater section). Pick up your ticket 15 minutes before the show.

Getting a ticket through a ticket agency (at most tourist offices or scattered throughout London) is quick and easy, but prices are inflated by a standard 20 to 25 percent booking fee. Ticket agencies are scalpers with an address. Agencies are worthwhile only if a show you've got to see is sold out at the box office. They scarf up hot tickets, planning to make a killing after the show is otherwise sold out. U.S.A.

booking agencies get their tickets from another agency, adding even more to your expense by involving yet another middleman.

Cheap theater tricks: Most theaters offer cheap returned tickets, standing room, matinee, and senior or student stand-by deals. Picking up a late return can get you a great seat at a cheap-seat price. Standing room costs only a few pounds. If a show is "sold out," there's usually a way to get a seat. Call and ask how. The famous "half-price booth" in Leicester (pronounced "Lester") Square sells cheap tickets to shows on the push list the day of the show only (14:30-18:30, Monday-Saturday). I usually buy the second-cheapest tickets directly from the theater box office. Many theaters are so small that there's hardly a bad seat. "Scooting up" later on is less than a capital offense. Shakespeare did it.

Royal Shakespeare Company—If you'll ever enjoy Shakespeare, it'll be here. (But lo, I've tried and failed.) The RSC splits its 12-play April-through-January season between the Royal Shakespeare Theatre in Stratford (tel. 01789/295623; recorded information tel. 01789/269191) and the Barbican Centre (open daily 9:00-20:00; credit-card booking, they mail out schedules; tel. 638-8891, tel. for recorded information: 628-2295). Tickets range in price from £8 to £22. For a complete schedule, write to the Royal Shakespeare Theatre, Stratford-upon-Avon, Warwickshire, CV37 6BB. Shakespeare fans stay tuned for the opening of the reconstructed Globe Theater (1996?) which will be doing Shakespeare as it was done in his day.

Music—For a fun classical event, attend a "Prom Concert." This is an annual music festival with almost nightly concerts in the Royal Albert Hall from July through September at give-a-peasant-some-culture prices (£3 standing-room spots sold at the door, tel. 589-8212). Look into the free lunchtime concerts popular in churches (listed at TI, especially Wren's St. Brides' Church, tel. 353-1301, and St. Martin-in-the-Fields, weekdays except Thursday at 13:05, tel. 930-1862).

The Ultimate Round of Beer—The London tube's Circle Line makes 21 stops during each orbit. There just happens to be a pub near the entry of each of these tube stops. A popular game is to race around trying to drink a pint (or a half-pint) at each of the 21 bars between the "old" pub hours (17:30 to 23:00). Twenty-one pints is about 2 gallons of beer. Locals prefer starting at the Farrington stop. A few of the pubs are tough to find—ask at the nearest newsstand for directions. (If you do this, send me a report.)

Sleeping in London
(£1 = about $1.50, tel. code: 0171)

London is expensive but there's no need to spend a fortune or stay in a depressing dump. Plan on spending about £50 (about $75) for a basic, clean, reasonably cheery double in a usually cramped, cracked-plaster building with an English (as opposed to continental) breakfast. Spending £34 gets you a double with breakfast in a safe, clean, tiny, dreary place where the landlords are absentee and service is minimal. (Hang up your towel to dry and reuse). My London splurges, at £70, are places you'd be happy to entertain in. Unless otherwise noted, the prices include a big English breakfast. Those traveling on a shoestring off-season save a few pounds by arriving late without a reservation and calling around.

I reserve my London room in advance with a phone call direct from the States (dial 011/44/171/London phone number). Assure the manager you'll arrive before 16:00, and leave your credit-card number as security. If you must send a deposit, ask if you can send a signed $100 traveler's check. (Leave the "pay to" line blank and include a note explaining that you'll be happy to pay cash upon arrival, so they can avoid bank charges, if they'll just hold your check until you get there.)

Sleep code: **S**=Single, **D**=Double/Twin, **T**=Triple, **Q**=Quad, **B**=Bath/Shower, **WC**=Toilet, **CC**=Credit Card (**V**isa, **M**astercard, **A**mex).

Sleeping in Victoria Station Neighborhood

The streets behind Victoria Station teem with budget B&Bs. It's a safe, surprisingly tidy and decent area without a hint of the trashy touristy glitz of the streets in front of the station. The first two listings are on Ebury street, between the train and coach stations, proudly part of Belgravia. Even with Margaret Thatcher living around the corner (you'll see the policeman standing outside #73 Chester Square), this is a

London, Victoria Neighborhood

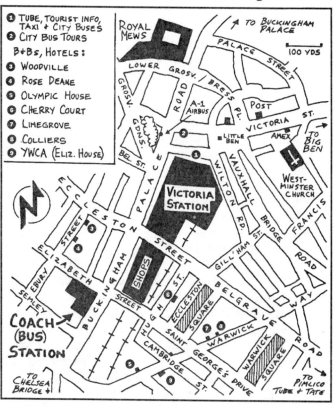

❶ TUBE, TOURIST INFO,
   TAXI + CITY BUSES
❷ CITY BUS TOURS

B+Bs, HOTELS:

❸ WOODVILLE
❹ ROSE DEANE
❺ OLYMPIC HOUSE
❻ CHERRY COURT
❼ LIMEGROVE
❽ COLLIERS
❾ YWCA (ELIZ. HOUSE)

classy and peaceful place to call home in London. Neighboring Elizabeth Street is the center for shops and eateries (#23 for take-out or eat-in fish and chips). The Duke of Wellington pub (63 Eaton Terrace, meals 18:00-22:30, not Sunday) is good, if smoky, for dinner. The cheaper listings are relatively dumpy. Don't expect £50 cheeriness in a £34 room. For the Warwick Way hotels, you might want to request a quiet back room. All are within a 5-minute walk of the Victoria tube and train station.

Woodville House is an oasis of small-town warmth and hospitality in downtown London. As in most budget hotels, the quarters are tight, but you'll get a small garden, homemade müesli, color-coordinated decor, orthopedic beds, showers down the hall, TVs in the room, a library, lots of travel tips, and endless tea, coffee, and friendly chat (especially about the local rich and famous) from the "extremely sociable, even at six in the morning" host Rachel Joplin and her husband Ian. (S-£36, D-£54; bunky family deals for three, four, or five in a room; easy credit-card reservations; 107 Ebury Street, Belgravia, SW1W 9QU, tel. 730-1048, fax 730-2574).

Rosedene Hotel, on the same fine street without the homey flair, is not as cramped as others in this price range. Its breakfast room doubles as a TV lounge (absentee owners but Saleha will take good care of you; S-£26, D-£35, T-£45, Q-£60; only a continental breakfast; CC:VM; 119 Ebury Street, SW1, tel. 730-4872, fax 224-6902).

Cherry Court Hotel is a minimal little place, plain, well-worn and cramped but very close to the station and offering eleven rooms at near-youth-hostel prices on a quiet street (SB-£25, D-£28, DB-£32, TB-35, Mrs. Patel promises these prices through 1995; toilets always down the hall; tea, coffee, and continental breakfast in your room; CC:VMA; 23 Hugh Street, SW1V 1QJ, tel. 828-2840).

Limegrove Hotel (S-£22, small D-£30, D-£32, T-£39, prices promised through 1995; 101 Warwick Way, SW1V 4HT, tel. 828-0458), carefully run by hard-working Joyce, is a little smoky and has only two toilets and two showers for nine rooms but is a fine value with TV and full English breakfast in the room. Back rooms are a bit quieter. **Colliers Hotel** (D-£32, DBWC-34; 97 Warwick Way, tel. 834-6931, fax 834-8439) next door, is a bit bigger with more showers but less personality. **Olympic House Hotel** (S-£30, D-£38; 115 Warwick Way, tel. 828-0757; run by Eddie and Betty) is a tall, skinny, claustrophobic tower of chaos with clean, quiet rooms and lots of steps.

Elizabeth House YWCA offers people of any sex inexpensive beds in a big, well-run, friendly, musty place with narrow yellow halls and stark rooms (S-£21, D-£42, DB-£45, shared T and Q-£15 per bed, with a buffet continental breakfast, request a quiet room off the street; 118 Warwick Way, SW1V 1SD, tel. 630-0741).

"South Kensington," He Said, Loosening His Cummerbund

For a chance to live on a quiet street so classy it doesn't allow hotel signs, surrounded by trendy shops and colorful eateries, 200 yards from the handy South Kensington tube station (on the Circle Line, direct connection to Heathrow, 2 stops from Victoria Station), call South Kensington home in London. Shoppers will enjoy the location, a short walk from Harrods and the designer shops of King's Road and Chelsea. You'll find plenty of ethnic and colorful budget eateries around the corner on Brompton Road (such as **La Bouchee**, daily 9:00-23:00, £8 French entrees). This has got to be the ultimate fairy-tale London home-away-from-home. Of course, you'll pay for it. But these places are a fine value.

Five Sumner Place Hotel is informal but professional, "highly commended" and recently voted "the best small hotel in London." You'll talk softly but not feel like you have to dress up as you wander, with your free daily newspaper, under the chandeliers out to the Victorian-style conservatory, a greenhouse dressed in blue, for breakfast. Each room is tastefully decorated with traditional period furnishings in a 150-year-old building (SBWC-£72, DBWC-£111, TBWC-£135, all with TV and telephone, elevator, CC:VMA, 5 Sumner Place, South Kensington, SW7 3EE, tel. 584-7586, fax 823-9962, if enough of you sleep here, maybe they'll give me a free room).

The Prince Hotel, right next door, is a bit smoky and relatively dumpy (but still nice). It also has an elegant, glass-covered conservatory, period decor throughout, and TVs and telephones in each of its 20 rooms. Its cheaper rooms ("without facilities," meaning with a shower but the toilet down the hall) are an especially good value (S-£42, SB-£48, SBWC-£61, DB-£61, DBWC-£74, TBWC-£92, QBWC-£108; breakfast in fancier hotel next door, 6 Sumner Place, SW7 3AB, CC:VMA, tel. 589-6488, fax 581-0824).

Aster House Hotel also offers you a chance to be elegant in London without going broke. The hotel's brochure reminds guests when they're going out to L'Orangerie (Victorian greenhouse) for breakfast, "To be considerate of your table companions, your neighbors and your hosts, we hope to welcome you in elegant attire, even if relaxed." Each room has a TV, telephone, fridge, and separate bathroom. Their third-floor rooms (no elevator) are the best deal. (SBWC-£61, third floor DBWC-£78, DBWC-£91, deluxe four-poster DBWC-£94 and £99, CC:VM, CC deposits non-refundable if you cancel with less than 2 weeks notice; entirely no smoking, 3 Sumner Place, SW7 3EE, tel. 581-5888, fax 584-4925). The breakfast room is whisper-elegant. Break the silence by asking who was scalded by their shower.

The **Uptown Reservations** B&B service has a line on 50 private homes renting classy rooms with breakfast in the "uptown" Chelsea, Knightsbridge, and Belgravia areas (S-37, D-£63, 50 Christchurch St. SW3 4AR London, tel. 351-3445, fax 351-9383). They also book flats and apartments. Monica and Sara work to match interests, so if you're an archaeologist or a coin collector, let them know.

Sleeping in Notting Hill Gate Neighborhood

Residential Notting Hill Gate is the perfect traveler's neighborhood. It has quick and easy bus or tube access to downtown, on the A2 Airbus line from Heathrow (second stop from airport, after Kensington Hilton), is relatively safe (except for the dangerous, riot-plagued Notting Hill Carnival, the last weekend of August), and, for London, is very "homely." Notting Hill Gate has a late-hours supermarket, self-serve launderette, artsy theater, and lots of fun budget eateries (see below). All recommendations are near the Holland Park or Notting Hill Gate tube station. (Notting Hill Gate is in the central zone and on the Circle Line, handier and 40p cheaper from anywhere in the center than the Holland Park station.)

Vicarage Private Hotel is understandably popular. Family-run and elegantly British in a quiet, classy neighborhood, it has 19 rooms furnished with taste and quality. Martin, Mandy, and Jim maintain a homey and caring atmosphere. Lots of stairs, a TV lounge, TVs in most rooms, and facilities on each floor. Reserve long in advance with a one-night deposit. (S-£32, D-£54, T-£66, Q-£72, a 6-minute walk from the Notting Hill Gate and High Street Kensington tube stations near Kensington Palace at 10 Vicarage Gate, Kensington, W8 4AG, tel. 229-4030).

London, Notting Hill Gate Neighborhood

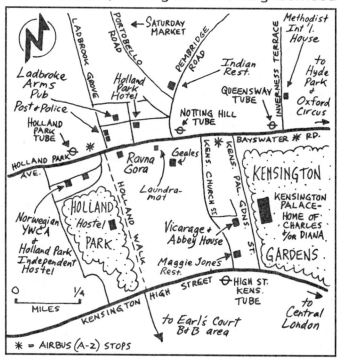

Abbey House Hotel, next door, is similar but has no lounge and is a bit less cozy (S-£32, D-£54, T-£64, Q-£74, Quint-£84; 11 Vicarage Gate, Kensington, W8, tel. 727-2594).

Hotel Ravna Gora—Formerly the mansion of 18th-century architect Henry Holland, now it's a large Yugoslavian-run B&B, eccentric and well-worn but comfortable, spacious, and handy for the price. Manda and Rijko take good care of their guests with a royal TV room and a good English breakfast (but no OJ). Plain, bright rooms; grand old creaky spiral staircase; easy parking (S-£28, D-£46, DB-£56, T-£54, TB-£66, Q-£68, QB-£80, CC:V; 50 yards from Holland Park tube station facing but set back from a busy road, 29 Holland Park Ave., W11, tel. 727-7725, fax 221-4282).

Dean Court Hotel—This wild and crazy Aussie hang-out offers young travelers good basic facilities (£11 beds in 3- to 5-bed rooms, D-£32, Twins-£35; 100 yards from Bayswater Tube, 57 Inverness Terrace, W2, reservations with deposit only unless one night before, tel. 229-2961, fax 727-1190).

Holland Park Hotel—Professional and "hotelesque," but a fine value. Royal lounge, sleepy garden, TVs in rooms, buffet continental breakfast, a little smoky, quiet, on a pleasant woodsy street, easy credit-card reservations (S-£38, SB-£47, D-£47, DB-£64, extra beds £12, CC:VMA; 6 Ladbrook Terrace, W11 3PG, tel. 792-0216, fax 727-8166).

Westend Hotel is comfortable and convenient but strict and without flavor (DB-£80, £68 in the annex, elevator in main building, all rooms with TV, telephone, hair dryer, coffee maker, and so on; CC:VMA, reserve with a credit-card number; 154 Bayswater Road, W2 4HP, tel. 229-9191, fax 727-1054).

Methodist International House—This Christian residence, filled mostly with Asian and African students, is great if you want a truly worldwide dorm experience at a price that will bolster your faith. Each smoke-free room is studious, with a desk and reading lamp. The atmosphere is friendly, safe, and controlled but well-worn with a silent study room, reading lounge, TV lounge, game room, and laundry facilities (£16 beds in shared doubles or triples, S-£20, D-£34, T-£48, includes breakfast and a cafeteria dinner—no typo; near Bayswater tube and a block from Queensway tube on a quiet street, 2 Inverness Terrace, W2 3HY, tel. 229-5101, fax 229-3170.)

Norwegian YWCA (Norsk K.F.U.K.)—For women under 25 only (and men with Norwegian passports), this is an incredible value—smoke-free; Norwegian atmosphere; on quiet, stately street; piano lounge, TV room, study; all rooms with private showers. They have mostly quads, so those willing to share with strangers are most likely to get a place. (July-August: SB-£24, bed in shared double-£21, shared quad-£16, with breakfast. September-June: same prices but with dinner included. Monthly rates-£11 a day in shared quad with breakfast and dinner. 52 Holland Park, W11 3R5, tel. and fax 727-9897). With each visit I wonder which is easier—getting a sex change or a Norwegian passport?

Holland Park Independent Hostel has spacious, ramshackle rooms; a TV lounge; no lockers; members' kitchen; and bugs (S-£13, D-£24, T-£33, bed in small unisex dorm-£9, no breakfast—and that's probably a blessing; 41 Holland Park, tel. 229-4238, 723-6833). On an aristocratic quiet street, it's a lovely alternative to the bushes.

Sleeping in London's Bloomsbury District

These places are between the British Museum and King's Cross Station, all within 3 blocks of the Russell Square tube station. **Cambria House**, an amazing value, is run by the Salvation Army. (Relax. This is a good thing when it comes to cheap big-city hotels.) This smoke-free old building with a narrow maze of halls is all newly painted and super clean—if institutional. The rooms are spacious and perfectly good. There are ample showers and toilets on each floor and a TV lounge (S-£23, D-£36, DBWC-£45, extra bed-£11, CC:VM; north of Russell Square at 37 Hunter Street, WC1N 1BJ, tel. 837-1654, fax 837-1229).

Repton Hotel is the cheapest and most run-down of several hotels on an elegant Georgian Terrace, a 2-minute walk from the British Museum. Prices may be soft and, with luck during slow times, you may get a dorm to yourself—in which case it's a great value. (S-£30, D-£40, DB-£56, 6-bed dorms-£12 per person, with a continental breakfast, TV in each room; 31 Bedford Place, WC1B 5JH, tel. 436-4922, tel. and fax 636-7045). **The Thanet** (D-£50, DBWC-£62, at #8 across the street, tel. 636-2869) is much nicer, but more expensive.

Central University of Iowa Hostel rents to non-Iowans from mid-May through August. It's clean, basic, and reminiscent of elegance with plenty of facilities (TV lounge, washer and dryer). (D-£32, beds in 3- to 4-bed rooms-£14, with continental breakfast; 7 Bedford Place, WC1B 5JA, tel. 580-1121).

Sleeping in Other Neighborhoods

Mary Ward's Guest House—Sleepable but very simple on a quiet street in a well-worn neighborhood south of Victoria near Clapham Common, this beats the hostel. Friendly Mary Ward (Edith Bunker's English aunt) has been renting her five super-cheap rooms to budget travelers for 25 years. (S-£10, D-£20 with English breakfast, 98 Hambalt Rd., Clapham Common, London, tel. 0181/673-1077, 15 minutes by tube to Clapham Common and a 12-minute walk—exit left down Chapham South Road, left on Elms, right on Abbeville Road, left on Hambalt.)

Lynwood Guest House—Outside of London (30 minutes by train) near Gatwick Airport (10 minutes by train), this place offers a cozy, friendly alternative to big-city lodging in Redhill, a normal workaday English town. Easy parking, a 5-minute walk from train station, owner Shanta may pick you up, genuinely caring and gracious (SB-£24, DB-£38, DBWC-£40, TB-£50, QB-£56; discount for 2 nights or more, 50 London Rd., Redhill, Surrey RH1 1LN, tel. 01737/766894).

The peaceful **Crutchfield Inn B&B** offers three comfortable rooms in a 500-year-old renovated farmhouse. Mrs. Blok includes a ride to and from the airport (DB-£45, 2 miles from Gatwick airport, 30 minutes by train from London, at Hookwood, Surrey, RH6OHT, tel. 01293/863110, fax 863233).

Eating in London

If you want to dine (as opposed to eat), check out the extensive listings in *What's On*. The thought of a £25 meal generally ruins my appetite, so my London dining is limited mostly to unremarkable, but inexpensive, alternatives. My listings are chosen mostly for their handy location to your B&B or sightseeing.

Your £5 budget choices are pub grub, a café, fish and chips, pizza, ethnic, or picnic. Pub grub is the most atmospheric budget option. Many of London's 7,000 pubs serve fresh, tasty buffets under ancient timbers, with hearty lunches and dinners priced around £5. Ethnic restaurants from all over the world more than make up for the basically lackluster English cuisine. Eating Indian or Chinese is "going local" in London. It's also going cheap (cheaper if you take out). Pizza places all over town offer £3.50 all-you-can-stomach buffets. Of course, picnicking is the fastest and cheapest way to go. There are plenty of good grocery stores and sandwich shops, fine park benches, and polite pigeons in Britain's most expensive city.

Eating near Trafalgar Square

For a meal on a monk's budget in an ancient crypt sitting on somebody's tomb, climb down into the **St.Martin-in-the-Fields Restaurant** (10:00-19:30, Sunday 12:00-15:00, £5-£7 cafeteria plates, cheaper sandwich bar, profits go to the church; underneath St. Martin-in-the-Fields on Trafalgar Square, tel. 839-4342). Down Whitehall (towards Big Ben), a block from Trafalgar Square, you'll find the atmospheric **Clarence Pub** (decent grub) and several cheaper cafeterias and pizza joints. For a classy lunch, treat your palate to the pricier **Brasserie** (first floor, Sainsbury Wing of the National Gallery).

Eating near Piccadilly

Wren at St. James Church Coffeehouse (8:00-19:00, Sunday 10:00-16:00, not exclusively vegetarian, 2 minutes off Piccadilly, at 35 Jermyn St., tel. 437-9419) is wonderfully green and in a pleasant garden next to one of Wren's best churches (peek in). **Stockpot** is famous and rightly popular for its edible cheap meals (8:00-23:30, Sunday 12:00-22:00, 40 Panton St., off Haymarket near Piccadilly). The palatial **Criterion Restaurant** (tel. 925-0909), serving a two-course dinner for £10 under gilded tiles and chandeliers, is 20 yards and a world away from the punk junk of Piccadilly Circus. **The Carvery** serves a £15 all-you-can-eat meaty buffet with plenty of vegetables and a salad bar, Yorkshire and bread pudding, dessert and coffee included—a carnivore's delight with concessions to vegetarians. Puffy-hatted carvers help you slice. (Regent Palace Hotel on Glasshouse St., a cigarette-butt toss from Piccadilly Circus, 12:00-14:30 and 17:15-21:00, Sunday 12:30-14:30 and 18:00-21:00).

Eating near Recommended Notting Hill Gate B&Bs

Costas has Greek food or eat-in or take-out fish and chips (£5 meals, closed Sunday, near the Coronet Theatre at Hillgate Street #18). Next door, the **Hillgate Pub** has good food and famous hot saltbeef sandwiches (indoor/outdoor, closed Sunday). The not-too-spicy **Modhubon** Indian restaurant is worth the moderate splurge (cheap lunch specials, 29 Pembridge Road, tel. 727-3399). There's a cheap Chinese take-out next door (19 Pembridge Road, 17:30-24:00, closed Sunday). The small, woodsy **Arc** at 122 Palace Gardens Terrace is popular and worth the moderate splurge (indoor-outdoor seating, £10-£15 meals, go early or call ahead, 18:30-23:15 nightly, tel. 229-4024). The **Churchill Arms** pub is a hot local hangout with good beer and decent

£5 Thai plates. The **Ladbroke Arms** serves country-style meals that are one step above pub grub in quality and price, daily from 12:00-14:30 and 19:00-21:30 (indoor/outdoor, 54 Ladbroke Road, behind Holland Park Tube station, tel. 727-6648). The almost-too-popular **Geale's** has long been considered one of London's best fish-and-chips joints (£6 meals, 2 Farmer Street, just off Notting Hill Gate behind the Gate Theatre, 12:00-15:00, 18:00-23:00, closed Sunday and Monday, tel. 727-7969). Get there early for a place to sit and the best selection of fish. The very English **Maggie Jones** (6 Old Court Place, just east of Kensington Church St., near the High Street Kensington tube stop, tel. 937-6462, CC:VM) serves my favorite £20 London dinner. If you eat well once in London, eat here.

Transportation Connections

Flying into London
At Heathrow Airport: Heathrow Airport is user-friendly. Read signs, ask questions. Most flights land at Terminal 3, but British Air flights land at Terminal 4 (same services as Terminal 3, but no tourist information office.) In Terminal 3, you'll find: **Banks** (open 24 hours daily, okay rates), airport terminal information desk (pick up a London map and ask questions, but for the official TI, see below), **car rental agencies** (if you're renting a car, stop by to confirm your plans), and a TI. Heathrow's TI (daily 8:30-18:00) gives you all the help that London's Victoria Station does, with none of the crowds. To reach the TI, walk 5 minutes following signs to the "underground." (If you're riding the Airbus into London, leave your partner at the terminal with your bags.) At the TI, get a free map and brochures, and buy a subway pass if you're riding the tube into London. Then either hop on the London-bound subway or walk back into the airport to catch the Airbus into London. The National Express Central Bus Station offers direct bus connections from the airport to Bath (every 2 hours, 2½-hour ride, tel. 0171/730-0202).

At Gatwick Airport: More and more flights, especially charters, land at Gatwick Airport, halfway between London and the southern coast. Trains shuttle conveniently between

Heathrow and the Four Terminals

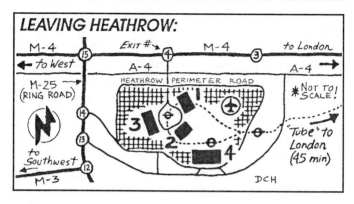

Gatwick and London's Victoria Station 4 times an hour (30-minute ride, £8.60).

When you fly to Europe, you lose a day. If you leave on Friday, you land on Saturday. Most flights from the U.S.A. arrive before noon.

Transportation to London from Heathrow Airport

By Tube (subway): For £3 (free with £4 all-day pass) the tube takes you 14 miles to Victoria Station in 45 minutes (6/hr).
By Airbus: Hop on a convenient Airbus (£5, 2/hr, 6:30-20:00, buy ticket on bus, tel. 0181/897-3305). All my recommended hotel neighborhoods are on one of the two Airbus lines. If you take A1, South Kensington is the third stop, and Victoria Station is the last stop. On A2, the second and third stops cover Notting Hill Gate, or stay on till the last stop, Russell Square, for Bloomsbury. The tube works fine, but with baggage I prefer taking the Airbus—no connections underground and a lovely view from the top of the double-decker bus. Ask the driver to remind you when to get off.
Taxis from the airport are expensive but rides from London to Heathrow can be reasonable. Locals can usually negotiate a £15 ride to Heathrow. Even at £20, for three traveling together this can be a deal.

Train and Bus Connections

Bath: Trains leave London's Paddington Station every hour (at a quarter after) for the 75-minute ride to Bath. The £26 tickets can be bought in advance or on the train from the conductor. For about the same price, you can take a guided bus tour from London to Stonehenge and Bath, and simply leave the tour in Bath.

Points North: Of course, London is the country's transportation hub. All of England is well-served from its capital. Speedy trains run hourly from London's King Cross Station stopping in York (2 hrs), Durham (3 hrs), and Edinburgh (5 hrs). For Cambridge connections, see below.

Transportation from London to Europe

While it's hard to nail down exact prices and options for those traveling from London to Paris or Amsterdam, it's safe to say that these routes are very competitive and you'll get better prices in London than from the U.S.A. Taking the bus is cheapest, and round-trips are a bargain. Flying is more reasonable than you might expect—students get great deals.

London to Paris—By bus: £33 one-way, £55 round-trip within six months, 10 hours, day or overnight, on Eurolines (tel. 0171/730-8235) or CitySprint (tel. 01304/240241). By train: £42 one-way overnight, £57 by day, 7 hours, £65 round-trip within five days, £85 round-trip within 2 months. BritRail Hover Speed crossing in 6 hours for £60. By plane: £90 regular, £40 student stand-by.

London to Amsterdam—By bus: £32 one-way, 12 hours, day or night, £53 round-trip within six months on Eurolines, same price to Brussels. By train: £50 one-way, day or night, 12 hours, £63 round-trip within five days, £83 round-trip within two months. The Jetfoil adds £9 to the ticket but cuts the channel crossing time from 4 to 1½ hours. To fly: £92 regular.

Near London: Cambridge

Cambridge, 60 miles north of London, is world-famous for its prestigious university. Wordsworth, Isaac Newton, Tennyson, Darwin, and Prince Charles are a few products of this busy brain-works. This historic town of 100,000 people is more pleasant than its rival, Oxford. Cambridge is the epitome of a university town, with busy bikers, stately residence halls, plenty of bookshops, and proud locals who can point out where electrons and DNA were discovered and where the first atom was split.

The university dominates—and owns—most of Cambridge. Approximate term schedule is January 15 through March 15, April 15 through June 8, and October 8 through December 8. The colleges are closed to visitors during exams, from mid-April until late June. But the town is never sleepy.

Planning Your Time

Cambridge is worth most of a day but no overnight. While Cambridge can be done between London and York, the cheap day-return train plan (£12.30, 2/hr, 60 min) makes Cambridge easiest and economical as a side trip from London. The budget ticket requires a departure after 9:30. You can arrive in time for the 11:00 or 12:00 walking tour (an essential part of any visit) and spend the afternoon in King's College, the Fitzwilliam Museum, and simply enjoying the ambiance of this stately old college town. Accommodations are frustrating in Cambridge.

Orientation (tel. code: 01223)

Cambridge is small but congested. There are two main streets separated from the river by the most interesting colleges. The town center has a TI, a colorful marketplace, and several parking lots. Everything is within a pleasant walk.
Tourist Info: The TI is on the town square (Monday-Friday 9:00-18:00 or 19:00; Saturday 9:00-17:00; summer Sundays 10:30-15:30; closed winter Sundays; tel. 322640).
Trains: To get to downtown Cambridge from the station, take a 20-minute walk, a £2.50 taxi ride, or an easy and fast-as-a-taxi "City Rail Link" shuttle bus (65p, every 8 minutes, direct to Emmanuel Street in front of the station).

Sights—Cambridge

▲▲**Walking Tour of the Colleges**—The best way to understand Cambridge's town-gown rivalry and to be sure of getting a good rundown on the historic and scenic highlights of the university—as well as some fun local gossip—is to take the walking tour. It's run by and leaves from the tourist office (July and August tours at 11:00, 12:00, 13:00, 14:00, and 15:00; the rest of the year, generally at 11:00 and 14:00). The 11:00,

13:00, and 14:00 tours spend a third of their time in King's College Chapel, which you could do on your own. Noon and 15:00 tours have more time for more variety. Tours cost £3.50 (or £5 for the ones that do KCC). You can drop by the TI early to grab a spot. Private guides are also available. Guide Friday hop-on and hop-off bus tours (£6, departing every 15 minutes) are informative and cover the outskirts, whereas walking tours go where buses can't: right in the center.

▲▲**King's College Chapel**—View the single most impressive building in town, high Gothic at its best, with the most medieval stained glass in any one spot, 2,000 tons of incredible fan vaulting and Rubens' great *Adoration of the Magi* (£2, erratic hours depending on school and events, but generally 9:30-16:30). During term you're welcome to enjoy the 17:30 evensong service (Tuesday-Saturday, 15:30 on Sunday).

▲▲**Trinity College**—Half of Cambridge's 63 Nobel Prize winners came from this richest and biggest of the town's colleges. Don't miss the Wren-designed library with its A+ architecture, wonderful carving, and fascinating original manuscripts (free, open Monday-Friday 12:00-14:00, Saturday 10:30-12:30). Just outside the library entrance, Sir Isaac Newton, who spent 30 years at Trinity, clapped his hands and timed the echo to measure the speed of sound as it raced down the side of the cloister and back. In the library you can read Newton's, hand-written account of this, alongside the original, hand-written *Winnie-the-Pooh*.

▲▲**Fitzwilliam Museum**—The best museum of antiquities and art outside of London, the Fitzwilliam has fine Impressionist paintings, old manuscripts, and Greek, Egyptian, and Mesopotamian collections (free; antiquities open Tuesday-Friday 10:00-14:00 and paintings 14:00-17:00; everything on Saturday 10:00-17:00 and Sunday 14:15-17:00; closed Monday; tel. 332900).

Museum of Classical Archeology—While this has no originals, it offers a unique chance to see accurate copies (from 19th-century casts of the originals) of virtually every famous ancient Greek and Roman statue (over 600 statues, free, 9:00-17:00 Monday-Friday, Sidgwick Ave., tel. 335153).

▲**Punting on the Cam**—For a little levity and probably more exercise than you really want, try hiring one of the traditional flat-bottom punts from stalls near either bridge and pole yourself up and down (around and around, more likely) the lazy Cam. Once you get the hang of it, it's a fine way to enjoy the scenic side of Cambridge. After 17:00, it's less crowded/embarrassing.

Transportation Connections

Cambridge to: London's Liverpool Station (2/hr, 60 min, £13.70 one-way or only £12.30 with a round-trip depart after 9:30 ticket). Cambridge to **York** (hrly, 2½-hour ride, with a transfer in Petersborough). By car, it's 60 high-speed miles (with no gas stations) on the M11 motorway to London. From Cambridge, any major road going west or south will direct you to the M11 motorway leading to the London ring road. Catch the poorly-marked M25 outer ring road (you'll see Heathrow and Gatwick signs) and circle around to the best position to start your central attack. (You can buy a good London map at the Cambridge TI for £1.) It's a 4-hour drive to **York** (take the more interesting A1 instead of the more tempting M1 motorway). Cambridge's huge, central Short Stay Parking Lot is handy.

BATH

Any tour of Britain that skips Bath stinks. Two hundred years ago, this city of 80,000 was the trend-setting Hollywood of Britain. If ever a city enjoyed looking in the mirror, Bath's the one. It has more "government listed" or protected historic buildings per capita than any other town in England. The entire city, built of creamy warm-tone limestone called "Bath stone," beams in its cover-girl complexion. An architectural chorus line, it's the triumph of Georgian style. Proud locals remind visitors that the town is routinely banned from the "Britain in Bloom" contest to give other towns a chance to win. Bath's narcissism is justified.

Promenade through the ages with a tour of Bath's Roman and medieval mineral baths, followed by tea and Vivaldi in the elegant Pump Room.

Planning Your Time

Bath is a two-night town even on a quick trip. There's plenty to do and it's a joy to do it. On a three-week British trip, I'd spend three nights in Bath with one day for the city and one for a side trip to Well, Glastonbury, and Avebury. Bath could easily fill another day. Ideally, use Bath as your jet lag recovery pillow (catching the bus directly from Heathrow airport, departures to "Bath Spa" at 10:30, 12:30, 14:30, 16:30; tel. 081/730-0202) and do London at the end of your trip.

Here's how I'd start a three-week British vacation:
Day 1: Land at Heathrow. Catch the National Express bus to Bath (depart every 2 hrs, 2½-hr trip). While you don't need or want a car in Bath, and most rental companies have an office there, those who pick up their cars at the airport can do Stonehenge (and maybe Salisbury) on their way to Bath on this day.
Day 2: 9:00, tour the Roman Baths; 10:30, catch the free city walking tour; 12:30, munch a picnic lunch on the open deck of a Guide Friday bus tour; 14:30, free time in the shopping center of old Bath; 16:00, take a guided tour through the Costume Museum.

Day 3: Pick up your rental car and tour Avebury, Glaston-bury (Abbey and Tower), and Wells (17:15 evensong at the Cathedral). Without a car, consider a one-day Avebury/Stonehenge/cute towns Mad Max minibus tour.

Day 4: 9:00, leave Bath early for South Wales; 10:30, tour St. Fagan's Folk Museum (grounds, lunch, then museum); 15:00, short stop at Tintern Abbey; drive to Cotswolds; 18:00, set up in your Cotswold homebase (Stow or Chipping). See below for more specifics on this day.

Orientation (tel. code: 01225)

Bath's town square, three blocks in front of the bus and train station, is a bouquet of tourist landmarks including the Abbey, the Roman and medieval baths, and the royal Pump Room.

Tourist Information

Near the Abbey (Monday-Saturday 9:30-18:00, Sunday 10:00-16:00, shorter hours off-season, tel. 462831). Pick up the 25p Bath map/guide and the packed-with-info, free *This Month in Bath*, and browse through scads of fliers.

Trains and Buses

The Bath Station is a pleasure (small-town charm and an international tickets desk). The bus station is immediately in front of the train station. My recommended B&Bs are within a 10- or 15-minute walk or a £2 taxi ride. For my top four listings, consider using the "Guide Friday" city bus tour (described below) as transportation. It leaves every 12 min-utes from Lane 1 of the bus station, a block in front of the train station. Start the tour, jump out, check into your B&B, and hop back on to finish the circle.

Sights—Bath

▲▲**The Guide Friday City Bus Tour**—This green-and-cream open-top tour bus makes a 90-minute figure-eight cir-cuit of Bath's main sights with an exhaustingly informative running commentary. For one £5.50 ticket, tourists can stop and go at will for a whole day. The buses cover the city cen-ter and the surrounding hills (14 sign-posted pick-up points, departures every 12 minutes in summer, hourly in winter, about 9:25-17:00, tel. 444102, children are often let on for

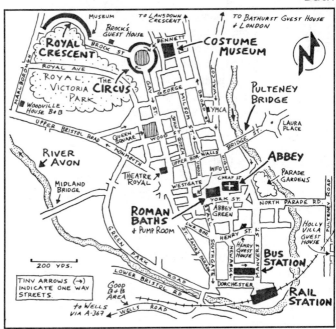

free). This is great in sunny weather, a feast for photographers, and a fine way to work on a tan and sightsee at the same time. The competing red Citytour buses (£4, family of 5 for £10) do basically the same tour without the swing through the countryside and ask the hard-to-answer question, "Why pay more?"

▲▲▲**Walking Tours of Bath**—These 2-hour tours, offered free by trained local volunteers who simply want to share their love of Bath with its many visitors, are a pure, chatty, historical-gossip-filled joy, essential for your understanding of this town's amazing Georgian social scene. How else will you learn that the old "chair ho" call for your sedan chair evolved into today's "cheerio" greeting? Tours leave from in front of the Pump Room daily except Saturday at 10:30 (often at 14:00 or 14:30 and 19:00, May-October). For Ghost Walks and Bizarre Bath Comedy Walks, see below under "Entertainment."

▲▲▲**The Baths (Roman and Medieval)**—Back in ancient Roman times, high society enjoyed the mineral springs at

Bath. Roman Londoners traveled to Aquae Sulis, as the city was called then, so often to "take a bath" that finally it became known simply as Bath. Today a fine Roman museum surrounds the ancient bath. With the help of an excellent 20-minute guided tour, the complex of ancient Roman and medieval baths and buildings makes sense. (£5; £6.60 "combo" ticket includes Costume Museum, a family combo costs £16. Open 9:00-18:00 daily, and 20:00-22:00 in August; slightly shorter hours off-season. Tours are included and leave on the quarter-hour throughout the day. Tel. 461111)

▲**Pump Room**—After a centuries-long cold spell, Bath was reheated when previously barren Queen Mary bathed here and ten months later bore a male heir to the throne (1687). Once Bath was back on the aristocratic map, high society soon turned the place into one big pleasure palace. The Pump Room, an elegant Georgian Hall just above the Roman baths, offers the visitor's best chance to sample this Old World elegance. Drop by to sip coffee or tea to the rhythm of a string trio (tea/coffee and pastry for £2.50, live music all year 10:30-13:00, summers 15:00-17:00). Now's your chance to have a famous (but not especially good) "Bath bun" and (split a 35p) drink of the awfully curative water. The Pump Room's toilets are always nearby and open to the discreet public.

▲**The Abbey**—Bath town wasn't much in the Middle Ages. As late as 1687, there were only about 3,000 inhabitants gathered around its great abbey. But an important church has stood on this spot since Anglo-Saxon times. In 973, Edgar, the first king of England, was crowned here. Dominating the town center, the present church is 500 years old and a fine example of Late Perpendicular Gothic, with breezy fan vaulting and enough stained glass to earn it the nickname "Lantern of the West" (concert and evensong schedule is on the door, worth the £1 donation, handy flier narrates a 19-stop tour). **The Heritage Vaults** (£2, 10:00-16:00, closed Sunday) is a small but interesting exhibit telling the story of Christianity in Bath since Roman times.

Pulteney Bridge—Bath is inclined to compare its shop-lined bridge to Florence's Ponte Vecchio. That's pushing it. But to best enjoy a sunny Bath kind of day, pay 60p to go into the garden below the bridge. Tour boats run hour-long £3.50 cruises from under the bridge.

▲▲**Royal Crescent and The Circus**—Bath is an architectural can-can and these are the kickers. These first elegant Georgian (that's British for "neoclassical") "condos" by John Wood are well-explained in the city walking tours. The museum at #1 Royal Crescent is your best look into a house from Jane Austen's day. It's worth the £3 admission to get behind all those classy exteriors (10:30-17:00, closed Monday, tel. 428126). Stroll the Crescent after dark. Pretend you're rich. Pretend you're poor. Study the cute little rooms below each entry walk. There're peasants on the lawn.

▲▲▲**Costume Museum**—One of Europe's great museums, displaying 300 years of fashion—from Anne Boleyn to Twiggy—one frilly decade at a time, is housed in Bath's elegant Assembly Rooms. Enthralling 45-minute tours will "knock your spots off." The tours normally leave on the hour or on the half-hour; drop by or call to confirm tour times. Learn why Yankee Doodle "stuck a feather in his cap and called it macaroni," and much more (£3.20, cheaper on combo ticket with Roman Baths, daily 10:00-17:00, from 11:00 on Sunday, last tour often at 16:00, tel. 461111).

▲▲**The Industrial Heritage Centre** is a grand title for Mr. Bowler's Business, a turn-of-the-century engineer's shop, brass foundry, and fizzy-drink factory. It's just a pile of meaningless old gadgets until a volunteer guide resurrects Mr. Bowler's creative genius (£3, plus a few pence for a glass of genuine Victorian lemonade, daily 10:00-17:00, 2 blocks uphill from the Assembly Rooms on Julian Rd., call to be sure a volunteer is available to give a tour, tel. 318348).

Small Special-Interest Museums: Building of Bath Museum offers a fascinating look behind the scenes at how the Georgian city was actually built. This is just one large room of exhibits but anyone interested in construction will find it worth the £2.50 (10:30-17:00, closed Monday, near the Circus on a street called "the Paragon," tel. 333895) **British Folk Art Collection** is also just one large room (next to the Building museum), offering a charming collection of crude but elegant folk art (£2, £3.50 combo ticket with Building Museum, tel. 446020). **Royal Photographic Society**, a hit with shutterbugs, exhibits the earliest cameras and photos and their development, along with temporary contemporary exhibits (£3, daily 9:30-17:30).

▲**American Museum**—I know, you need this in Bath like you need a Big Mac. But this offers a fascinating look at colonial and early-American lifestyles. Each of 18 completely furnished rooms (from the 1600s to the 1800s) is hosted by an eager guide waiting to fill you in on the candles, maps, bedpans, and various religious sects that make domestic Yankee history surprisingly interesting. One room is a quilter's nirvana (£5, Tuesday-Saturday 14:00-17:00, Sunday 11:00-17:00, closed November-March, tel. 460503). The museum is outside of town and a headache to reach without a car (15-minute walk from the Guide Friday stop or a 10-minute walk from bus #18).

Shopping—There's great browsing between the Abbey and the Assembly Rooms. Shops close at 17:30, later on Thursdays. Interested in antiques? For the best deal, pick up the local paper (usually out on Fridays) and shop with the dealers at estate sales and auctions listed in the "What's On" section.

Entertainment—*This Month in Bath* (available at the TI and many B&Bs) lists events and evening entertainment. There are almost nightly historical walks (19:15, 2 hrs). For a walking comedy act, the entertainingly off-the-wall Bizarre Bath walk is a kick (£3, 20:00 nightly, 75 minutes, from the Huntsman pub near the Abbey, confirm at TI or call 335124). Ghost Walks are another way to pass the after-dark hours (20:00, 2 hrs, £3, tel. 463618). The Bath Sports and Leisure Centre (just across the North Parade Bridge, open until 22:30, tel. 462563) has a swimming pool and more.

Sleeping in Bath
(£1 = about $1.50, tel. code: 01225)

Bath is one of England's busiest tourist towns. To get a good B&B, make a telephone reservation in advance. Competition is stiff and it's worth asking any of these places for a nonweekend, three nights in a row, or off-season deal. Friday and Saturday nights are tightest (especially if you're staying only one night, since B&Bs favor those staying longer).

Sleep code: **S**=Single, **D**=Double/Twin, **T**=Triple, **Q**=Quad, **B**=Bath/Shower, **WC**=Toilet, **CC**=Credit Card (Visa, Mastercard, Amex).

Brock's Guest House—If you can afford the splurge, this Georgian townhouse will put bubbles in your Bath experience. Marion Dodd has redone her place in a way that would make the famous architect John Wood, who built it in 1765, proud. This charming house couldn't be better located, between the prestigious Royal Crescent and the elegant Circus (S-£22, DB-£42 and £44, DBWC-£48 and £52, TB-£55, TBWC-£66; 32 Brock St., BA1 2LN, reserve far in advance, tel. 338374, fax 334245). Marion serves a royal breakfast. You'll find a TV and teapot in your room, and a launderette around the corner. Like most listings in this book, she'll hold telephone reservations with no deposit until 15:00 (call if you'll be a little late). If Marion's place is full, she can set you up in a friend's B&B nearby. If you can't find a sedan chair, Marion is a 15-minute walk, £2.50 taxi, or short bus ride (to Assembly Rooms and short walk) from the station. Guide Friday buses stop on Brock Street.

In the **Woodville House**, Anne and Tom Toalster offer Bath's best cheap beds. This tidy little house has three charming rooms, one shared shower, and a TV lounge. Breakfast is a help-yourself buffet around one big family-style table (D-£27, minimum 2 nights; just off busy Bristol Road below the Royal Crescent at 4 Marlborough Lane, BA1 2NQ, tel. 319335, absolutely no smoking).

Elgin Villa (DB-£30, DBWC-£36 for 2 nights minimum with this book promised through 1995; next door to Woodville House at 6 Marlborough Lane, BA1 2NQ Bath, tel. 424557), run by Rex and Edie Haldenby, has three rooms and serves a big continental breakfast in your bedroom.

Holly Villa Guest House, with a cheery garden and a cozy TV lounge, an 8-minute walk from the station and center, is enthusiastically and thoughtfully run by Jill McGarrigle. (D-£34, DB-£38, DBWC-£46, T-£48, TB-£60, Q-£56, double rooms have double beds only, seven rooms, non-smoking, free parking, cheap rooms get the famous "loo with a view." From city center, walk over North Parade Bridge, take first right, then second left, a block from a Guide Friday bus stop, 14 Pulteney Gardens, BA2 4HG, tel. 310331.)

The **Henry Guest House** is a clean, cheery, and vertical little 8-room family-run place 2 blocks in front of the train station on a quiet side street (S-£16, D-£32, T-£48, TVs in rooms, lots of narrow stairs, one shower and one bath for all; 6 Henry Street, BA1 1JT, tel. 424052, Mrs.

Cox). This kind of decency at this price this central is found nowhere else in Bath. **Harington's of Bath Hotel**, with 12 rooms on a quiet street in the town center, is sleepable in a pinch (D-£40, DB-£46, family room deal, CC:VMA, Queen Street, tel. 461728).

The Bathurst Guest House—Mrs. Elizabeth Tovey runs a fine B&B (S-£16.50, D-£33, DB-£38, extra bed-£8, non-smoking, TVs in rooms, lots of stairs, easy parking, 11 Walcot Parade, London Road, Bath BA1 5NF, tel. 421884) with a great piano/game lounge, 1 block above the A-4 London Road about a 15-minute walk north of the town center. The friendly **Claremont B&B** is farther out of town (D-£32, DB-£40, T-£50; 9 Claremont Rd., Bath, Diane Harding, tel. 428859).

For the cheapest beds, the **Youth Hostel** is in a grand old building, but not central (bus #18 from the station, £8.40 per bed without breakfast, tel. 465674). The **YMCA** is a bit grungy, but friendly and wonderfully central on Broad Street. Doubles are £12 per person; the dorm is cheaper at about £11, with breakfast (tel. 460471).

Eating in Bath

Bath is flooded with cutesy eateries. There's something for every appetite and budget—just stroll around the center of town. A picnic dinner or take-out fish and chips in the Royal Crescent Park is ideal for aristocratic hobos.

Eating on or just off the Abbey Green

Evans Self-Service Fish Restaurant is the best eat-in or take-out fish and chips deal in town (11:30-22:00, closed Sunday, 7 Abbeygate, student discounts, tel. 463981). The **Crystal Palace Pub**, with hearty meals under rustic timbers or in the sunny courtyard, is a good handy standby (meals under £5, daily from 12:00-14:30 and 18:00-20:30, 11 Abbey Green; children welcome on the patio, not indoors; tel. 423944). **Sally Lunn's House** is a cutesy quasi-historic place for expensive doily meals, tea, pink pillows, and lots of lace (4 North Parade Passage). **The Huntsman** (next to Sally Lunn's buns, tel. 460100) offers good, filling meals. Its pub is cheapest, the Cellar Bar is inexpensive and full of young locals, and the restaurant upstairs is a bit classier. For very cheap meals, try **Spike's Fish and Chips** (open very late) and the neighboring café just behind the bus station.

Eating between the Abbey and the Circus

For lunch, try **Lovejoy's Café** upstairs in the Bartlett Street Antique Centre or the **Green Tree Pub**, with a non-smoking room, on Green Street (both serve lunch only, downhill from the Assembly Rooms). The Guildhall Market across from the Pulteney Bridge, fun for browsing and picnic shopping, has a very cheap cafeteria if you'd like to sip tea surrounded by stacks of used books, bananas on the push list, and honest-to-goodness old-time locals. The **Broad Street Bakery** (at 14 Broad St.) is a budgetricious place with great quiches and pizzas to eat in or take away. **Devon Savouries** serves greasy, delicious take-out pasties; sausage rolls; and vegetable pies (on the main walkway between New Bond Street and Upper Borough Walls). **Sam Wellers Pub** serves good £5 dinners (open until 20:00, closed Sunday, 14 Upper Borough Walls, tel. 466627).

Eating near the Circus and Brock's Guesthouse

The **Circus**, on Brock Street, is intimate and a good value with candle-lit prices. The **Cedars Lebanese Restaurant** (on a lane called Margaret's Buildings, just off Brock Street) serves an elegant have-it-all £12 "Cedars Mezze." A block or so away, the **Chequers Inn** (50 Rivers St.) is a smoky dive of a pub with cheap and finger-sticking disgusting grub.

Transportation Connections

Bath to London: Trains to London's Paddington station (hrly, 90 minutes, £26 one-way), National Express buses are cheaper (hrly, 3 hrs, £18 round-trip, £17 one-way, ask about £7 cheap day returns). Consider using an all-day Stonehenge and Bath organized **bus tour** from London as transportation to Bath. For the same cost of the train ticket (£25), you can see Stonehenge, tour Bath, and leave the tour before it returns to London (they'll let you stow your bag underneath). Direct National Express **buses** run between Heathrow airport and Bath (9 daily, 2½ hrs), and Gatwick and Bath (8 daily, 4½ hrs, change at Heathrow). Public transportation is such a snap that it's better to rent a **car**

in Bath than rent a car in London and drive to Bath. Most major car rental companies have offices in Bath and offer free hotel pick-ups.

The Cotswolds: National Express **buses** (tel. 01272/541022) run between Bath and various destinations in the Cotswolds, such as **Cheltenham** (4 daily, 2 hrs), **Stratford** (2 daily, 3 hrs), and nearby **Oxford** (3 daily, 2 hrs).

Birmingham, points north: From Bath, catch a **train** to **Bristol** (twice hourly, 15-minute ride) and from Bristol to **Birmingham** (hrly, 1½ hrs). From Birmingham, a major transportation hub, trains depart for **Blackpool**, **York**, **Durham**, and **Scotland**, or use a train and bus combination to reach **Ironbridge Gorge**, **North Wales**, and the **Lakes District**.

Near Bath: Glastonbury, Wells, Avebury, Stonehenge, and South Wales

Oooo, mystery, history. Glastonbury is the ancient home of Avalon, King Arthur, and the Holy Grail. Nearby medieval Wells gathers around its grand cathedral where you can enjoy an evensong service. Then get neolithic at every Druid's favorite stone circles, Avebury and Stonehenge.

An hour east of Bath, at St. Fagan's Welsh Folk Museum, you'll find South Wales' traditional story vividly told in a park full of restored houses. Relish the romantic ruins of Tintern Abbey, the lush Wye River Valley, and the quirky Forest of Dean.

Planning Your Time

Everybody needs to see Stonehenge. But I'll tell you now, it looks just like it looks. You'll know what I mean when you pay to get in and rub up against the barbed wire that keeps us at a distance. It's great, but Avebury is the connoisseur's circle: more subtle and welcoming. Each are worth an hour. Avebury is better. Wells is simply a cute town, much smaller and more medieval than Bath, with a bombshell of a cathedral that's best experienced at the 17:15 evensong service. Glastonbury is normally done surgically (in 2 hrs): see the abbey, climb the tower and scram. Avebury, Glastonbury, and Wells make a wonderful day out from Bath. Splicing in Stonehenge is possible but stretching it.

Think of the South Wales sights as a different grouping. Ideally, they fill the day you leave Bath for the Cotswolds. Anyone interested in Welsh culture can spend 4 hours in the St. Fagan's Folk museum. Castle-lovers and romantics will want to consider the Caerphilly Castle, Tintern Abbey, and Forest of Dean (each a worthwhile quick stop). See above for proposed day-by-day schedule.

Getting Around

Wells, Glastonbury, and the major sights in South Wales are easily accessible by bus from Bath; the Badgerline offers a "Day Rambler" ticket (£4.50, £9 per family, tel. 01225/464446). Avebury and Stonehenge are trickier. The most convenient, quickest way to see Avebury and Stonehenge without a car is to take an all-day bus tour. Several tours leave from Bath, and Maddy Thomas' are cheapest and most fun.

Maddy Thomas runs all-day 6-to-12-person **"Mad Max" tours** (£12) in her comfortable new 14-seater minibus. She thoughtfully organizes informative and inexpensive countryside excursions from Bath on most days. Her schedule flexes according to demand. She picks up almost daily at 8:45 (at the statue on Cheap Street, behind Bath Abbey) for her basic all-day "Avebury, Stonehenge, and two cute villages (Lacock and Castle Combe)" tour. Maddy is an authority on the region's history and mystery. For the latest on this tour and on Maddy's similar one-day tours of the Cotswolds and Dartmoor, get her schedule at the Bath TI or call the Bath hostel (tel. 465674) or Brock's Guest House (tel. 338374).

For another inexpensive personable local guide with a car or minibus, contact Jodi Nicholls in Bath at tel. 01373/831311. (Jodi is an American who often assists her husband, Roy Nicholls, when he leads Best of Britain in 22 Days minibus tours for my company, Europe Through the Back Door, featuring the destinations in this book.)

By car, you'll encounter good roads. In a day, you could easily do a loop trip from Bath to Avebury (25 miles) to Glastonbury (56 miles) to Wells (6 miles) and back to Bath (20 miles). If you're low on time, stick to the faster "A" roads to go as directly as possible. A loop trip from Bath to South Wales is roughly 100 miles.

Glastonbury

This place, located on England's most powerful line of pre historic sights (called a "ley" line), gurgles with history and mystery. While the town is a curious mix of Benny Hill and Benny Hinn, most visitors do the sights and skip today's lowbrow/New Age Glastonbury. As you climb the legend-soaked conical hill called Glastonbury Tor, notice the remains of the labyrinth. In A.D. 37, Joseph of Arimathea brought vessels containing the blood and sweat of Jesus to Glastonbury, and with that, Christianity to England. While this is "proven" by fourth-century writings and accepted by the Church, the Holy Grail legend which sprang from this in the Middle Ages isn't. Many think the Grail trail ends at the bottom of the "Chalis Well," a natural spring at the base of the Glastonbury Tor.

In the 12th century, England needed a morale-boosting folk hero for inspiration during a war with France. The fifth-century Celtic fort at Glastonbury was considered proof enough of the greatness of the fifth-century warlord Arthur. His supposed remains were dug up from the Abbey floor, and Glastonbury Tor became woven into the Arthurian legends.

The Glastonbury Abbey was England's most powerful in the tenth century. In the 16th century, Henry VIII, recognizing Glastonbury as a bastion of the church he fought, destroyed the Abbey. For emphasis, he hung and quartered the Abbot, sending the parts of his body to four different towns. Not to be kept down for more than a few centuries, Glastonbury rebounded. In an 18th-century tourism campaign, thousands signed affidavits stating that water from the Chalis Well healed them, and once again Glastonbury was on the tourist map. Today Glastonbury and its Tor are a center for searchers, too creepy for the mainstream church, but just right for those looking for a place to charge their crystals. The Tor is seen by many as a Mother Goddess symbol.

Climb the Tor and visit Chalis Well at its base (great view, easy parking, always open), tour the Abbey (£2, daily 9:30-18:00, evocative ruins with an informative visitor center and a model of the church in the chapter house, tel. 01458/ 832267), and browse through the town. The **Rainbow's End** café (2 minutes from the Abbey on High Street) is a fine place for salads and New Age people-watching.

If you're looking for a midwife or a male-bonding tribal meeting, check the notice board. (TI tel. 01458/32954.)

From Bath, buses run hourly to Wells (1½ hrs). Transfer at Wells for Glastonbury (25 min).

Wells

This wonderfully preserved little town has a cathedral, so it can be called a city. It's England's smallest cathedral city, with one of its most interesting cathedrals. Don't miss the 13th-century carving on the west front, the unique hour-glass-shaped double arch inside, or the grand chapter house (daily 7:15-19:00 or dusk, hour-long tours at 10:30, 11:00, 11:30, 14:00 and 14:30 except on Sunday, good shop and a handy cafeteria, tel. 674483). Weekdays (except Wednesday) at 17:15 and Sundays at 15:00, the cathedral choir takes full advantage of the place's heavenly acoustics with a 30-minute evensong service.

For a fine cathedral-and-town view from your own leafy hilltop bench, hike 10 minutes up Tor Hill. Lined with perfectly pickled 14th-century houses, the oldest complete street in Europe is Vicar's Close, 1 block north of the cathedral. Also next door is the moated Bishop's Palace (£2, open daily in August 11:00-18:00; April-October Tuesday and Thursday 11:00-18:00 and Sunday 14:00-18:00; closed in winter).

If you're in the mood for a picnic, drop by an aromatic cheese shop for a great selection of tasty local cheeses. Remember, Cheddar is just down the road. Ask the lady for a pound's worth of the most interesting mix. The Wells TI is on the Main Square (tel. 01749/672552). Buses run hourly between Wells and Bath (1½ hrs).

Sleeping and Eating: Wells is a pleasant overnight stop. The **Tor Guest House**, with 8 rooms in a 17th-century building facing the east end of the cathedral, is a good value (D-£35, DB-£45; cozy lounge and breakfast room; quiet, friendly, with car park; 20 Tor St., BA5 2US, tel. 01749/672322). The nearby **Fountain Inn**, on St. Thomas Street, is the best place for pub grub (fine curry, spareribs, and draft cider). The **City Arms Pub** is fun if you fancy grub in a former medieval jail.

Sights—Near Wells

▲**Wookey Hole**—This tacky commercial venture, worthwhile maybe as family entertainment, is a real hodgepodge. It starts with a wookey-guided tour of some big but mediocre caves complete with history, geology lessons, and witch stories. Then you're free to wander through a traditional rag paper-making mill with a demonstration, and into a 19th-century circus room—a riot of color, funny mirrors, and a roomful of old penny-arcade machines that visitors can actually play for as long as their pennies (on sale there) last. They even have old girlie shows. (£5.60, daily May-September 9:30-19:00, last ticket 90 minutes before closing, October-April 10:30-16:30, 2 miles east of Wells, tel. 01749/672243.)

Wilkins Cider Farm—Scrumpy is the wonderfully dangerous local hard cider brewed in this part of England. The traditional old Wilkins Cider Farm, in Mudgeley near Wells, welcomes visitors. Apples are pressed from September through December. A half-gallon costs £2.40.

Avebury and Stonehenge

▲▲**Avebury**—The stone circle at Avebury is bigger (16 times the size), less touristy, and I think more interesting than Stonehenge. You're free to wander among 100 stones, ditches, mounds, and curious patterns from the past, as well as the village of Avebury, which grew up in the middle of this fascinating 1,400-foot-wide Neolithic circle.

Take the 1-mile walk around the circle. Visit the fine little archaeology museum (skip the one on local farm life) and pleasant Stones café next to the National Trust store. The Red Lion Pub has good, inexpensive pub grub (and does B&B, D-£35, tel. 01672/539266). Notice pyramid-shaped Silbury Hill just outside of Avebury. Nearly 5,000 years old, this largest manmade object in prehistoric Europe is a reminder that you've just scratched the surface of Britain's prehistoric and religious landscape.

▲▲**Stonehenge**—England's most famous stone circle, with parts older than the oldest pyramid, was built between 3100 and 1100 B.C. These huge stones were brought all the way from Wales to form a remarkably accurate celestial calendar. Even today, every summer solstice (around June 21) the sun sets in just the right slot and Druids boogie. The monument is roped off, so even if you pay the £3 entry fee, you're kept at a distance. You can see it free from the road (daily 10:00-18:00).

South Wales

▲**Cardiff**—The Welsh capital has 300,000 people and a pleasant modern center across from the castle. A visit is interesting only if you catch one of the entertaining tours (every half-hour). The interior is a Victorian fantasy. Reach Cardiff from Bath by train (runs hourly, 1½ hrs with change in Bristol).

▲▲▲**Welsh Folk Museum at St. Fagan's**—This best look at traditional Welsh folk life displays more than 20 carefully reconstructed old houses from all corners of this little country. Each is fully furnished and comes equipped with a local expert warming herself by the toasty fire and happy to tell you anything you want to know about life in this old cottage. Ask questions! You'll see traditional crafts in action and a great gallery displaying crude washing machines, the earliest matches, elaborately carved "love spoons," and even a case of memorabilia from the local man who pioneered cremation. Everything is well explained. St. Fagan's has three sections: houses, museum, and castle/garden. If the sky's dry, see the houses first. Spend an hour in the large building's fascinating museum, and skip the castle and gardens. The museum's cafeteria, the Vale Restaurant, is inexpensive and excellent. (£4, daily 10:00-17:00, closed winter Sundays, tel. 01222/ 569441.) City buses run frequently between Cardiff and St. Fagan's Welsh Folk Museum.

▲**Caerphilly Castle**—This impressive but gutted old castle, 30 minutes from the Welsh Folk Museum, is the second-largest in Europe (after Windsor). With two concentric walls, it was considered to be a brilliant arrangement of defensive walls and moats. Notice how Cromwell's demolition crew tried to destroy it, creating the leaning tower of Caerphilly (£2, daily 9:30-18:30, shorter hours in winter).

▲**Tintern Abbey**—Just off the scenic A466 road in a lush natural setting, this poem-worthy ruined Abbey is worth a stop. The helpful TI and shop has the useful Wye-Cotswolds map and Wales Tourist Board's *A Tourist Guide to North Wales* for sale.

▲**Wye River Valley and Forest of Dean**—Lush, mellow, and historic, this region seduced me into an unexpected night in a castle. Local tourist brochures explain the Forest of Dean's special dialect, strange political autonomy, and its oaken ties to Trafalgar and Admiral Nelson.

For a medieval night, check into the **St. Briavel's Castle Youth Hostel** (members only, tel. 01594/530272). An 800-year-old Norman castle used by King John in 1215, the year he signed the Magna Carta, it's comfortable (as castles go), friendly, and in the center of the quiet village of St. Briavels just north of Tintern Abbey. For dinner, eat at the hostel or walk "just down the path and up the snyket" to the **Crown Pub** (good, cheap food and friendly pub atmosphere).

Route Tips for Drivers

From Bath to South Wales: Leave Bath following signs for A4, then M4, then Stroud. It's 10 miles north (on A46 past a village called Pennsylvania) to the M4 super-freeway. Zip westward, crossing a huge suspension bridge into Wales. Twenty miles farther, just past Cardiff, take Exit 33 and follow the brown signs south to the Welsh Folk Museum. To reach Tintern Abbey from St. Fagan's, take M4.

From Cardiff to Cotswolds via Forest of Dean: Just before the big suspension bridge, take Chepstow Exit #22, and follow signs up A466 to Tintern Abbey and the Wye River Valley. Carry on to Monmouth and, if you're running late, follow the A40 and the M50 to the Tewksebury exit, where small roads will take you into the Cotswolds.

THE COTSWOLDS

The Cotswold Hills, a hilly 25-by-50-mile chunk of Gloucestershire, are dotted with storybook villages and graced with England's greatest countryside palace, Blenheim.

As with many fairy-tale regions of Europe, the present-day beauty of the Cotswolds was the result of an economic disaster. The area grew rich on the wool trade and built lovely towns and houses. ("Cotswold" comes from the Saxon phrase meaning "hills of sheeps' coats.") Then foreign markets stole the trade and the towns slumped—too poor even to be knocked down. These forgotten, time-passed villages have been rediscovered by us 20th-century romantics, and the Cotswolds are enjoying new prosperity.

Nestled in the heart of the Cotswolds are two of its coziest towns: Stow-on-the-Wold and Chipping Campden. Either village makes an ideal home base for your exploration of the thatch-happy Cotswolds.

Planning Your Time

The Cotswolds are an absolute joy by car (and a royal headache without one). With a car, on a three-week British trip, I'd spend two nights and a day in the Cotswolds (sleeping in Stow or Chipping Campden). Consider this 100-mile day—but only with a good local map:

9:00 Joyride through Chipping Campden, Broadway, and Stanton, then drive via Cheltenham to Cirencester.

11:00 Cirencester for its Corinium Museum, crafts center, and lunch.

13:00 Drive to Bibury via Coln St. Dennis, Coln Rogers, and Coln Powell.

13:30 Bibury for a stroll along the stream, cottages, and church.

14:30 Drive to Blenheim via Burford, Witney, and Woodstock.

15:15 Line up for the hour-long tour of Blenheim Palace

17:15 Drive to Stow-on-the-Wold via Chipping Norton.

18:00 Evening Stroll around Stow or Chipping Campden.

19:30 Find a good pub for dinner if you're not in Stratford for a play.

Drivers will get an early start the next morning, leaving the Cotswolds for their Stratford/Warwick/Ironbridge Gorge day.

Getting Around the Cotswolds

Trains get you only to the fringes of the Cotswolds. Buses cover the interior erratically. Pick up the small *Cotswolds Bus and Rail Guide* at any bus or train station. Consider renting a bike for a more intimate look at the Cotswolds. For a quick visit, consider Moreton-in-Marsh or Cheltenham (train info: 014525/29501, bus info: 511655) as home bases. Both are located on major rail lines and have bus connections to Cotswolds villages. Moreton-in-Marsh, linked by bus to Chipping Camden, has a lively, colorful market on Tuesday. If you want just a taste of the Cotswolds, take a tour from Bath to Castle Combe, the charming southernmost

Cotswolds Villages and Surroundings

Cotswold town. (Ask at Bath TI for info about Mad Max and Guide Friday tours.)

Sights—The Cotswolds

▲**Stow-on-the-Wold**—Eight roads converge on Stow-on-the-Wold, but none interrupt the peacefulness of its main square. Stow has become a crowded tourist town but most are day-trippers, so even summer nights are peaceful. Stow has no real sights other than itself, a cutesy huddle of medieval pastel boutiques, good pubs, pleasant shops, and art galleries draped seductively around a big town square. At the TI on the main square (tel. 01451/831082), get the handy little 20p walking tour brochure called "Town Trail" (also sold at youth hostel). A visit to Stow is not complete until you've locked your partner in the stocks on the green. For accommodations, see Sleeping, below.

▲**Chipping Campden**—Nine miles north of Stow and less touristy, Chipping Campden is a working market town, home of some incredibly beautiful thatched roofs and the richest Cotswold wool merchants.

Walk the full length of High Street (its width is characteristic of market towns) and around the block on both ends. On one end you'll find impressively thatched homes on Westington Street, past Sheep Street, and on the other end, a fine 15th-century perpendicular "wool" church and a pleasant free memorial garden.

The bizarre and pathetic tourist office is located on High Street in a 600-year-old building shared with the quirky "Woolstaplers' Hall Museum" (wooden legs, old typewriters, jelly molds, and the "largest collection of iron man-traps in Europe"). The TI and museum are open daily 10:00-17:00 (tel. 01386/840289 or 840101, 5p town maps). For accommodations, see Sleeping, below.

▲**Cirencester**—Nearly 2,000 years ago, this was the ancient Roman city of Corinium. It's 20 miles from Stow down A429, which was called Foss Way in Roman times. In Cirencester (towns ending in "cester" were Roman camps), stop by the Corinium Museum to find out why they say, "If you scratch Gloucestershire, you'll find Rome" (£1.25, 10:00-17:00, Sunday 14:00-17:00, shorter hours and closed Monday off-season). The cutesy crafts center and workshops entertain visitors with traditional weaving, baking, potting in action, an interesting gallery and a good coffee shop. Friday is market day in Cirencester (TI tel. 01285/654180).

Bourton-on-the-Water—I can't figure out if they call this the "Venice of the Cotswolds" because of its quaint canals or its miserable crowds. It's too cute, worth a drive-through and a few cynical comments, but no more (4 miles south of Stow).

Broadway—Another very crowded town, worth a drive-through but not a stop. There won't be a parking place, anyway (9 miles northwest of Stow).

▲**Stanton and Upper and Lower Slaughter**, between Stow and Broadway, are my nominations for the cutest Cotswold villages. They nestle side by side in equally beautiful countryside. Ask your dad if you can sit on the roof as you drive past the stone walls, oaks and sheep. Get out of your car and walk around.

▲**Bibury**—Six miles northeast of Cirencester, this is an entertaining but money-grubbing and not-very-friendly village with a trout farm, a Cotswolds museum, a stream teeming with fat trout and proud ducks, a row of very old weavers' cottages, and a church surrounded by rose bushes, each tended by a volunteer of the parish. Don't miss the scenic drive from A429 to Bibury through the villages of Coln St. Dennis, Coln Powell, and Winson. Drivers can drop passengers in Coln Rogers for a pleasant 2-mile walk into Bibury, where devoted drivers will have an idyllic stream-bank picnic awaiting the walkers.

▲▲▲**Blenheim Palace**—Too many English palaces can send you into a furniture-wax coma. Visiting one is enough . . . as long as it's Blenheim. The Duke of Marlborough's home, the largest in England, is still lived in. That is wonderfully obvious as you prowl through it. The palace is well-organized with mandatory, excellent guided tours that leave every 10 minutes, last an hour, and cost £7. Winston Churchill was born prematurely while his mother was at a Blenheim Palace party. If you need more time in the excellent Churchill exhibit, skip to the next tour group (mid-March to October 10:30-17:30, last tour at 16:45, tel. 0993/811325). Churchill fans can visit his tomb, a short walk away, in the Bladon town churchyard. The train station nearest Blenheim Palace is Hanborough, on the Worcester-Oxford train line.

▲**Woodstock**—Blenheim Palace sits at the edge of this cute town, stealing the show. For a half-timbered and memorable splurge, the **Star Inn** (DB-£45, CC:VMA, Market Place, OX20 ITA Woodstock, tel. or fax 01993/811373), a 5-minute walk from the palace, is good for an overnight.

▲**Hidcote Manor**—If you like gardens, the grounds around this manor house are worth a look. These gardens, among the best in England, are at their fragrant peak in May, June, and July (£5, 11:00-19:00, no entry after 18:00, closed Tuesday and Friday, just past Chipping Campden).

Sleeping in the Cotswolds
(£1 = about $1.50)

Sleeping in Stow-on-the-Wold (tel. code: 01451)
My first three listings are comfortable modern homes just outside town, a 5-minute walk from the square. The next three are old buildings right on the square. The last one is in a tiny village a 10-minute drive away.

Sleep code: **S**=Single, **D**=Double/Twin, **T**=Triple, **Q**=Quad, **B**=Bath/Shower, **WC**=Toilet, **CC**=Credit Card (**V**isa, **M**astercard, **A**mex).

The Croyde B&B—Norman and Barbara Axon make you feel like part of the family. They offer two rooms, each with a double bed, in a pleasant, quiet, modern house with a garden, easy parking, and a warm and friendly welcome (D-£30, on Evesham Rd., Stow-on-the-Wold, Cheltenham, GL54 1EJ, tel. 831711). If my listings are full, Barbara can find you a good place elsewhere.

West Deyne B&B—Mrs. Joan Cave runs this cozy B&B with a peaceful garden overlooking the countryside on Lower Swell Road (double or twin-£30 with evening tea and biscuits, GL54 1LD, tel. 831011).

The Limes is run by Val Keyte, who's hosted travelers for nearly 20 years and serves a great breakfast (D-£32, DB-£34, DBWC-£36, family rooms and a four-poster bed, across the street from the Croyde B&B, on Evesham Rd., GL54 1EJ, tel. 830034).

The Pound—In her comfy, quaint, restored 500-year-old low-ceilinged, heavy-beamed home, Patricia Whitehead offers two spacious bright rooms with good strong twin beds and a classic old fireplace lounge (D-£32, right downtown on Sheep St., GL54 1AU, tel. 830229).

Stow Lodge Hotel, on the town square in its own sprawling and peaceful garden next to the church, is the best friendly, classy, old-hotel value. Thoughtfully appointed rooms in the main building are quieter and more characteristic than in the annex (DB-£72, TB-£94, CC:A, no elevator, GL54 1AB, tel. 830485). They have two simple £52 doubles that they keep strapped to a bedpost in the attic. This is a large but family-run hotel that somehow maintains a happy staff.

Stow-on-the-Wold Youth Hostel—On Stow's main square in a historic old building, with a friendly atmosphere, good hot meals served and a do-it-yourself members' kitchen, it's popular in summer. Call-in reservations are held until 18:00, or later with a credit card number (£6.50 per bed, £4 for dinner, tel. 830497). Other Cotswold Youth Hostels are in Cleve Hill (tel. 0124267/2065) and Duntisbourne Abbots (tel. 01285821/682).

The Guiting Guest House—Six miles west of Stow in the tiny village of Guiting Power, this is a sleepy-village alternative. Mrs. Sylvester rents modern, delightfully doily rooms in her 400-year-old house (DB-£39, Post Office Lane, Guiting Power, Cheltenham, GL54 5TZ, tel. 01451/850470). Her husband is the local tourist board's B&B quality control man, so this place is either right on...or gets away with murder.

Sleeping in Chipping Campden (tel. code: 01386)

Frances Cottage—Jill Slade rents two comfy rooms in her small home (DB-£34, £32 for stays of more than 1 night, 1 triple, non-smoking, narrow stairs, Lower High Street, GL55 6DY, tel. 840894).

Sparlings B&B—Those in search of aristocratic tidiness and grandfatherly clocks will sleep well in the very proper Mr. Black and Mr. Douglass' delightfully restored 17th-century stone town house. (D-£42, DB-£44, 1 night's deposit required, peaceful garden, on High Street, GL55 6HL, tel. 840505).

Eating in the Cotswolds

In Stow, the formal but friendly bar in the **Stow Lodge** serves fine £5 lunches and £7 dinners (daily noon-14:00,

19:00-21:00). Next door, the **Queen's Head** serves an inexpensive decent meal and the local Cotswold brew, Donnington Ale (closed Monday). Near Stow, try dinner at **The King's Head** in Bledington (moderate, closed Sunday). **The Plough**, in the hamlet of Cold Aston (a 10-minute drive from Stow), is known for its good typical Cotswold food and atmosphere.

In Chipping Campden, the **Volunteer Pub** is your best cheap bet (Lower High Street, £5 lunch or dinner, 19:00-21:00). The **Badgers Wine Bar** serves better food with less smoke for around £8 (in town center, on High Street). For a lively local crowd and very likely a little impromptu folk music, everyone loves the **Baker's Arms** for dinner (closed Sunday, in Broad Campden, near Chipping Campden). Since things change constantly, take your B&B host's pub-grub advice seriously.

Train Connections

The heart of the Cotswolds is connected to the nearest train lines by sporadic buses. Use the *Cotswolds Bus and Rail Guide* (free, at train and bus stations) to plan your arrival and departure. When leaving the Cotswolds, catch a bus to the nearest train line (either Cheltenham or Moreton-in-Marsh) and continue your journey. **London-Oxford** (2/hr, 1½ hr), **Cheltenham-Bath** (hrly, 1 hr, easy change in Bristol), **Cheltenham-Birmingham** (hrly, 45 min). Birmingham, a major transportation hub, is your jumping-off point for Ironbridge Gorge, North Wales, northern England, and Scotland.

Near the Cotswolds: Stratford, Warwick, and Coventry

Shakespeare's hometown, Stratford . . . to see or not to see? A walking tour with a play's the thing to bring the bard to life in this touristy town. Explore Warwick, England's finest medieval castle, and stop by Coventry, a workaday town with a spirit the Nazis couldn't destroy.

Planning Your Time

Stratford, Warwick, and Coventry are a made-to-order day for drivers connecting the Cotswolds with Ironbridge Gorge or North Wales. While connections from the Cotswolds and to IBG are tough, Stratford, Warwick, and Coventry are well connected by public transportation.

Stratford is a classic tourist trap. But since you're passing through, it's worth a morning. (Don't spend the night. A play is an easy commute the night before from the Cotswolds.) Warwick is England's single most spectacular castle. Very touristy but fun for three hours, it has good cafeteria and picnic facilities. Coventry, the least important stop on a quick trip, is most interesting as an opportunity to see a real, struggling, workaday north-English industrial city (with some decent sightseeing).

The area is worth only a one-day drive-through. If you're speedy, hit all three sights. If you're more relaxed, do Stratford and Warwick and get to your Ironbridge Gorge B&B in time to enjoy the evening ambiance of that more-interesting stop.

Getting Around

Buses and trains connect Stratford, Warwick, and Coventry (bus tel. 01788/535555). For example, Stratford and Warwick towns are linked by both buses and trains (nearly hrly, 20-min ride). London-Stratford is 2½ hrs by train, 3 hrs by bus. Driving is easy: Stow to Stratford (20 miles) to Warwick (8 miles) to Coventry (10 miles).

Stratford-upon-Avon

▲▲**Shakespeare's Birthplace**—Stratford is the most over-rated tourist magnet in England, but nobody back home would understand if you skipped Shakespeare's house. In the town center (address unnecessary, follow crowds, TI-tel. 01789/293127), this half-timbered Elizabethan building is furnished as it was when young William grew up there and is filled with bits about the life and work of the great dramatist (£2.60, 9:00-18:00, from 10:00 on Sunday, shorter hours in winter).

Shakespeare's hometown is blanketed with opportunities for "Bardolatry." There are four other "Shakespearian properties," all run by the Shakespeare Birthplace Trust, in and near Stratford. Anne Hathaway's Cottage, a mile out of town in Shottery, is a picturesque thatched cottage in which the bard's wife grew up. Much more than a "cottage," it's a 12-room farmhouse that has little to do with Shakespeare but offers an intimate peek at lifestyles in Shakespeare's day. Guides in each room do their best to lecture to the stampeding hordes. Mary Arden's House, the girlhood home of William's mom, is in Wilmcote, about 3 miles from town. This 16th-century farmhouse sees far fewer tourists, so the guides in each room have a chance to do a little better guiding. A 19th-century farming exhibit and a falconry demonstration are on the grounds (both houses, about the same hours and price as His birthplace).

▲▲**Guide Friday Stratford Tours**—These open-top buses constantly make the rounds, allowing visitors to hop on and hop off at every sight in town. The full circuit takes about an hour and comes with a steady and informative live commentary (£6.50, buses every 15 minutes from 9:30, less frequent off-season, tel. 01789/294466).

▲▲**Walking Tour**—A far better value than touring the various Shakespeare buildings, a guided walk makes this historic but oversold town endearing. Tours are scheduled only on Sundays at 10:30 (£2, starting where Shakespeare did), but private tours are affordable for small groups. Call Mrs. Pat Bouverat at 01789/269890.

The World of Shakespeare is a gimmicky but fun look at Elizabethan and Renaissance England (£3.50, 9:30-21:30 in summer, until 17:30 in winter, shows on the half hour, 25-minute show, between the big Theatre and the bridge/TI, tel. 01789/269190).

▲▲**Royal Shakespeare Company**—The RSC, undoubtedly the best Shakespeare Company on earth, splits its season between London and Stratford. If you're a Shakespeare fan, see if the RSC schedule fits into your itinerary either here or in London. Tickets range from £7-£33 (Monday-Saturday at 19:30, Thursday and Saturday matinees at 13:30). You'll probably need to buy your tickets in advance, although 50 seats are saved to be sold each morning, and unclaimed tickets can often be picked up the evening of the show (box office tel. 01789/295623, 24-hour ticket availability information tel. 01789/269191). Theater tours are given most days at 13:30 and 17:30, but not on matinee days. Over a thousand RSC paintings, props and costumes are on display (9:15-

20:00, Sunday 12:00-17:00). The Shakespeare Connection is a convenient rail/bus shuttle for Stratford playgoers sleeping in London (2½ hours each way, £25 round-trip). If you have a car, Stow and Chipping Campden are only 30 minutes from Stratford and an evening of classy entertainment. If you don't like Shakespeare, attending a play out of guilt will change nothing and be just an expensive waste of time.

Warwick and Coventry

▲▲**Warwick Castle**—England's finest medieval castle is almost too groomed and organized, giving its hordes of visitors a good value for the steep £6.75 entry fee. With a lush, green, grassy moat and fairy-tale fortification, Warwick will entertain you from dungeon to lookout. There's something for every taste—a fine and educational armory, a terrible torture chamber, a knight in shining armor posing on a horse, a Madame Tussaud re-creation of a royal weekend party with an 1898 game of statue-maker, a grand garden, and a peacock-patrolled, picnic-perfect park (daily 10:00-18:00, 80-minute cassette tape tours for £1.50, sandwiches on sale in park, best castle eatery is The Stables near the turnstile, tel. 01926/445421).

▲**Coventry's Cathedral**—The Germans bombed Coventry to smithereens in 1940. From that point on, the German word for "to really blast the heck out of a place" was to "coventrate." But Coventry rose from the smithereens, and its message to our world is one of forgiveness and reconciliation. The symbol of Coventry is the bombed-out hulk of its old cathedral with the huge new one adjoining it. The inspirational complex welcomes visitors. Climb the tower (1,180 steps). If you're touring the church, first see the 18-minute movie, *The Spirit of Coventry*, downstairs (£1.25 for the movie, plus a requested donation at the church door, 9:30-17:00, Sunday 11:30-15:30, tel. 01203/227597).

Coventry's most famous hometown girl, Lady Godiva, rode bareback through the town in the 11th century to help lower taxes. You'll see her bronze statue a block from the cathedral (near Broadgate). Just beyond that is the Museum of British Road Transport (first, fastest, and most famous cars and motorcycles from this British "Detroit"). Browse through Coventry, the closest thing to normal workaday urban England you'll see. (TI tel. 01203/832303.)

Route Tips for Drivers

Entering Stratford from the Cotswolds, you cross a bridge. Veer right (following "P," Wark, and Through Traffic signs) and park in the multi-story garage in the center of town (50p, 2 hrs, you'll find nothing easier or cheaper). The TI and Guide Friday bus stop are just a block away. Theaters and Shakespeare's house are 4 blocks away. Leaving the garage, circle to the right around the same block but stay on the "Wark" (Warwick, A46) road. Warwick is 8 miles away. The castle is just south of town on the right. After touring the castle, carry on through the center of Warwick, following signs to Coventry (still A46). If stopping in Coventry, follow signs painted on the road into the "city centre" and then to cathedral parking. Grab a place in the high-rise car park. Leaving Coventry, follow signs to Nuneaton and M6 North through lots of sprawl and you're on your way. The M6 threads through giant Birmingham. Form M6, take M54 to the Telford/Ironbridge exit. Following the Ironbridge signs, you do-si-do through a long series of roundabouts until you're there.

IRONBRIDGE GORGE

The Industrial Revolution was born in the
Severn River Valley. In its glory days, this
now-drowsy valley gave the world the first
iron wheels, steam-powered locomotive,
and cast-iron bridge. The great museums in
the town of Ironbridge Gorge will take you back into those
heady days when Britain was racing into the modern age and
pulling the rest of the West with her.

Planning Your Time

On a short trip without a car, IBG isn't worth the headaches.
By car I'd slip it in between the Cotswolds/Stratford/War-
wick and North Wales. For the shortest reasonable visit,
arrive in the early evening to browse the town and spend the
morning and early afternoon touring the sights here before
driving on to North Wales (e.g. 10:00, Visitors' Centre;
11:00, Blists Hill Museum for a picnic, cafeteria, or pub
lunch and sightseeing; 15:30, drive to Wales via Llangollen).

Speed demons could zip in for a midday tour of Blists
Hill and a look at the bridge, and speed out. With a month
in Britain, I'd spend two nights and a more leisurely and
complete day that includes the Coalbrookdale museums.

Orientation (tel. code: 01952)

The town gathers within 3 or 4 blocks of the iron bridge that
spans the Severn River. The actual museum sites are scattered around within a couple of miles.

Tourist Info: A block from the iron bridge (8:45-18:00, weekends from 10:00, off-season closing at 17:00, tel. 432166).

Getting Around: In late July and August there may be a
cheap shuttle bus between all sights. Otherwise, those without wheels are in for a walk. The sights are within a 2-mile
radius. Drivers will find things well signposted.

Sights—Ironbridge Gorge

▲▲▲**Ironbridge Gorge Industrial Revolution
Museums**—Start with the Iron Bridge. The first ever (1779),
this is the valley's centerpiece, open all the time, free, easy,
and thought-provoking.

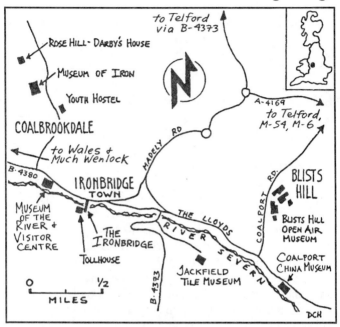

The **Museum of the River and Visitors' Centre**, in the Severn Warehouse 500 yards upstream, is the orientation center. Start your visit here (opens at 10:00) to see the 10-minute introductory movie, check out its exhibit and model of the gorge in its heyday, and buy your guidebook and tickets (£8 for the Ironbridge Passport to all the sights, £6 for Blists Hill only).

Just up the road in **Coalbrookdale**, you'll find the Museum of Iron (worth a quick look) and Abraham Darby's blast furnace (inside a glass pyramid). This is the birthplace of the Industrial Revolution where, in 1709, Darby first smelted iron using coke as fuel. If you're like me, "coke" is a drink and "smelt" is the past tense of smell, but this event kicked off the modern industrial age.

Save most of your time and energy for the great **Blists Hill Open-Air Museum**—50 acres of Victorian industry, factories, and a re-created community from the 1890s, complete with Victorian chemists; an ancient dentist's chair; candlemakers; a working pub; a fascinating squatter's cottage;

and a snorty, slip-slidey pigsty. Take the lovely walk along the canal to the "inclined plane" and have a picnic, or lunch in the Victorian Pub or the cafeteria near the squatter's cottage. The £1.25 Blists Hill guidebook gives a good step-by-step rundown (daily 10:00-17:00, maybe until 18:00 in summer, tel. 01952/433522 on weekdays, 432166 on weekends).

Sleeping in Ironbridge Gorge
(£1 = about $1.50, tel. code: 01952)
Sleep code: **S**=Single, **D**=Double/Twin, **T**=Triple, **Q**=Quad, **B**=Bath/Shower, **WC**=Toilet, **CC**=Credit Card (Visa, Mastercard, Amex).

The Hill View Farm—While Rosemarie Hawkins runs a peaceful, clean, friendly farmhouse B&B, her husband John raises a "beef suckler herd." Walk around the farm. If the gander's out, wear your jeans. If you're looking for calm and country, this is it, in a great rural setting overlooking the ruins of a 12th-century abbey (S-£16, double-£30, twin-£32; Buildwas, Ironbridge, Shropshire, TF8 7BP; tel. 432228). The Hawkins' farm is halfway between Ironbridge and Much Wenlock on A4169; leave Ironbridge past the huge modern power plants (coal), cross the bridge, and go about a mile. You'll see the sign.

The Library House is "better homes and castles" elegant. In the town center, right across from the bridge, it's classy but friendly, and a fine value. Chris and George Maddocks run a smoke-free place. Their breakfast won a "healthy heartbeat" award. (DB-£44, TB-£55; 11 Severn Bank, 1B, Shropshire TF8 7AN, tel. 432299, easy telephone reservations, they can reserve a table for you at the Coracle restaurant, parking passes available.)

The Wharfage Cottage is not cramped but cozy, a comfy three-bedroom place with ancient beams and color TVs, run by Pat Sproson (D-£36, DB-£38, TB-£50, QB-£56; 17 the Wharfage, TF8 7AW, on "main street," 2 minutes from the bridge, easy parking, tel. 432721).

Severn Lodge offers three rooms in an 1832 captain-of-industry mansion with a sit-a-spell garden and views of the lush hills (but not of the river where the sweatshops used to groan). This spacious place has all the hotel extras and easy parking. Carefully playing by the tourist board rules,

Mrs. Reed won the coveted "Deluxe" (top 1%) category. (Twin or double with the works-£46; from the Wharfage Cottage, go 1 block up the small steep New Road, Ironbridge, Shropshire, TF8 FAX, tel. and fax 432148).

Woodlands Farm is an adventure in budget sleeping. When local workers aren't housed here, the musty, shaggy-carpeted but sleepable place offers the cheapest beds in town (S-£10, D-£20, DB-£25, T-£30, with an English breakfast; from the IBG Museum's Visitor Centre, take the steep little road about a mile, Beech Road, tel. 432741). The farm runs a private fishing business, Beeches Pool, where only barbless hooks are used and locals toss their catch back to hook again (kind of a fish hell).

Ironbridge Gorge Youth Hostel—Built in 1859 as the Coalbrookdale Institute, this grand building is now a fine hostel (a 20-minute walk from the Iron Bridge down A4169 toward Wellington, £9 beds with sheets in 4- to 6-bed rooms, £4 dinners, closed from 10:00-17:00, easy telephone reservations, tel. 433281).

Wilderhope Manor Youth Hostel—This beautifully remote and haunted 500-year-old manor house is one of my favorite youth hostels anywhere in Europe. One day a week, tourists actually pay to see what we youth hostelers sleep in for £8. Closed Sunday night. It's 6½ miles from Much Wenlock down B4371 toward Church Stretton. Evening meals are served at 19:00 (tel. 01694/771363).

Eating in Ironbridge Gorge
The Coracle Restaurant, run by Mr. and Mrs. Prichard, is every local's favorite place for a special evening out (£7 dinners, 19:00-21:30, closed Sunday and Monday, reservations normally necessary; town center, near the bridge, tel. 433913). Downstairs, Peter and Paul run **Oliver's**, a delightful smoke-free vegetarian place.

For a pleasant evening, drive down Wenlock Edge on B4371. At the **Wenlock Edge Inn**, park and walk to the cliff for a marvelous view of Shropshire at sunset. Also good are the entertaining **George and Dragon Pub** and the **Talbot Pub** in Much Wenlock and the **Meadow Inn** (which won the "best food in the country" award) near the power stacks just west of Ironbridge Gorge.

Transportation Connections

Public transportation is miserable. Buses (every 2 hrs) and cabs run the 7 miles between Ironbridge and the nearest train station at Telford. The Telford bus and train stations are a 15-minute walk apart. **Trains from Telford to: Birmingham** (hrly, 45 min), **Blackpool** (Birmingham-Shrewsbury-hrly, 60 min; Shrewsbury-Crew-hrly, 40 min; Crew-Preston-2/hr, 45 min; Preston-Blackpool-2/hr, 20 min), **Lakes District** (Preston-Penrith 2/hr, 75 min, and bus into Keswick), **Edinburgh** (8 hrs, with several changes).

Driving in from the Cotswolds and Stratford, take M6 through Birmingham, then M54 to the Telford/Ironbridge exit. Following the Ironbridge signs, you do-si-do through a long series of roundabouts until you reach Ironbridge Gorge.

NORTH WALES

North Wales offers up a real Welsh stew: a medieval banquet, a mighty castle, giant slate mines, and some of Britain's most beautiful scenery in the Snowdonia National Park. From towering Mount Snowdon to lush forests to desolate moor country, North Wales is a poem written in landscape. Ruthin is the perfect home base for your exploration.

Planning Your Time

North Wales is worth two nights and a day on a 3-week British trip. With a car, I'd set up in Ruthin and do the following loop through this fascinating chunk of North Wales:

9:00   Drive to Caernarfon with short stops in Trefriw Mill, Betws-y-Coed (info centre, shops, waterfall), and over Llanberis Mountain Pass.

12:00   Caernarfon Castle. Catch noon tour, 13:00 movie in Eagle Tower. See Prince Charles (of Wales) exhibit. Climb to top for view. Walk through Caernarfon town, shop.

14:30   Drive the scenic road to Blaenau Ffestiniog.

15:30   Tour Llechwedd Slate Mine.

17:30   Drive home to Ruthin.

19:00   Arrive back in Ruthin.

20:00   Medieval banquet at castle (if not last night).

On a quick trip without a car, Ruthin isn't worth the trouble Train in to Bangor where you can catch a bus to Caenarfon (2/hr). From Caenarfon you can bus to Llanberis and Blaenau.

Getting Around North Wales

North Wales is best covered by a combination of buses and trains. Pick up schedules at any station in North Wales, and ask about Rover and Ranger passes. The Crewe-Holyhead train, running east and west, stops at Llandudno Junction (where you can catch a southbound train to Betws-y-Coed and Blaenau Ffestiniog, 6/day) and at Bangor (where you can catch a bus to Caernarfon, 2/hr). Unfortunately, this destination is great for drivers and puts others at a serious disadvantage.

North Wales

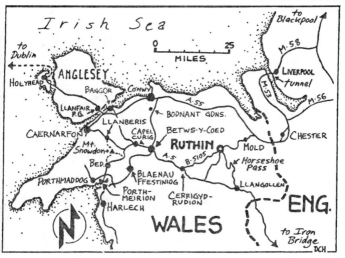

If you are in Ruthin without wheels: To get to Caernarfon, first take a bus to the handiest train station at Rhyl (hrly, 75 min). From Rhyl, catch the train west to Bangor, then catch a bus south to Caernarfon (4/hr, 25 min). To reach Betws-y-Coed and Blaenau Ffestiniog from Ruthin, get to Rhyl by bus, then catch a train to Llandudno Junction (2/hr, 20 min). At the Junction, transfer to a train heading south to Betws-y-Coed (6/day, 30 min) and Blaenau Ffestiniog (30 more minutes).

Ruthin

Ruthin (rith-in), a market town serving the scenic Vale of Clwyd (klu-id), is a low-key workaday town whose charm is in its ordinary Welsh-ness. Its market square, castle, TI, bus station, and the in-town accommodations are all within 5 blocks of each other. I stop here because it's as Welsh as can be, makes a handy base for drivers doing North Wales, and it serves up a great medieval banquet. The TI office (daily 10:00-17:30 in summer, shorter hours off-season, tel. 01824/703992) is in a busy crafts center with 13 working shops, a gallery, and a fine cafeteria. (For accommodations, see Sleeping, below.)

Ruthin

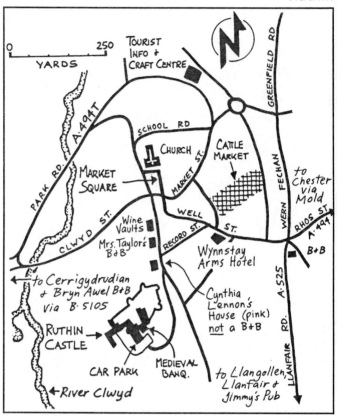

▲▲The Ruthin Castle Welsh Medieval Banquet—All "medieval banquets" are touristy gimmicks. This one is really fun and culturally justifiable (if that's necessary). For one crazy evening, take a romanticized trip into the bawdy Welsh past. English, Scottish, Irish, and Welsh medieval banquets are all variations on the same theme. This one is more tasteful and less expensive than most.

You'll be greeted with a chunk of bread dipped in salt, which the maiden explains will "guarantee your safety." Your medieval master of ceremonies then seats you, and the evening of food, drink, and music rolls gaily on. Harp music, angelic singing, wenches serving mead, spiced wine, four hearty traditional courses eaten with your fingers and a dagger, bibs, candlelight, pewter goblets, and lots of entertainment, including insults slung at the Irish, Scots, English, and even us brash colonists. (£23, vegetarian options, starts at 20:00, runs most nights depending upon demand, down Castle Street from the town square, easy doorstep parking, CC:VMA, call for reservations, tel. 01824/703435.)

Llangollen

Worth a stop if you have a car, Llangollen is famous for its musical International Eisteddfod (for six days starting the first Tuesday in July; July 4-9 in 1995), a festival of folk songs and dance, very popular—and crowded. You can walk or ride a horse-drawn boat down its old canal (£3, 45-min round-trip, tel. 01978/860702) toward the lovely 13th-century Cistercian Vale Crucis Abbey (£1.50) near the even older cross called Eliseg's Pillar. (TI tel. 01978/860828.) Llangollen is a 30-minute drive from Ruthin. Hourly buses connect Llangollen with train stations at Chirk and Wrexham.

▲**Welsh Men's Choir**—For an informal evening of great Welsh singing, visitors are welcome at the Hand Hotel (inexpensive pub dinners, but don't sleep here, tel. 01978/860303) in Llangollen. Practice sessions start at 19:30 on Monday and Friday, followed by a sing-along in the pub at 21:00. Warning: the hotel may be filled with large tour groups.

Betws-y-Coed

This is the resort center of Snowdonia National Park, bursting with tour buses and souvenir shops. It has a good National Park and Tourist Information office (tel. 01690/710426). The main street is worth a walk.

As you drive west out of town on A5, you'll see the car park for scenic Swallow Falls, a 5-minute walk from the road. A mile or so past the falls, on the right, you'll see "The Ugly House," built overnight to take advantage of a 15th-century law that let any quickie building avoid fees and taxes. A regular bus service connects Conwy and Betws-y-Coed. Trains run from the north coast through Betws-y-Coed to Blaenau (6/day).

Trefriw Woolen Mills—The mill in Trefriw, 3 miles north of Betws-y-Coed, is free and surprisingly interesting

(Monday-Friday 9:00-12:00 and 14:00-17:30, tel. 01492/ 640462). Follow the 11 stages of wool manufacturing—warping, weaving, carding, hanking, spinning, and so on; then enjoy the fine woolen shop, pleasant town (more so than Betws-y-Coed), and coffee shop.

Caernarfon

This small but powerful-feeling town bustles with shops, cafés, and people. The TI across from the castle entrance (tel. 01286/672232) can nearly always find you an inexpensive B&B. The **Isfryn B&B** is a good value (S-£16.50, D-£32, DB-£37, family deals, 11 Church St., tel. 01286/ 675628). It's just down the street from the castle, overlooking the water.

▲▲**Caernarfon Castle**—Edward I built this impressive castle 700 years ago to establish English rule over North Wales. It's a great castle, all ready to entertain. Watch the movie (on the half-hour in the Eagle Tower); climb the Eagle Tower for a great view; take the guided tour (50-min tours for £1 leave on the hour from the center of the courtyard in front of entry—if you're late, ask to join one in progress); and see the special exhibit on the investiture of Prince Charles and earlier Princes of Wales (£3.50, daily 9:30-18:30, winter 9:30-16:00, Sunday 11:00-16:00, tel. 01286/677617).

Blaenau Ffestiniog

This quintessential Welsh slate-mining town (TI tel. 01766/830360) is notable for its slate-mine tour. The **Fron Heulog Guest House** is friendly, offers discount coupons to the Llechwedd mines, and can point you toward the chapel where the men's choir rehearses (D-£25, High Street, tel. 01766/831790, Keith and Liz Thomasson).

▲▲**Llechwedd Slate-Mine Tour**—Slate mining played a huge role in Welsh heritage, and this mine on the northern edge of the bleak mining town of Blaenau Ffestiniog does its best to explain the mining culture of Wales. This is basically a romanticized view of the depressing existence of Victorian-age Welsh miners who mined and split most of the slate roofs of Europe. For every ton of usable slate found, 10 tons are mined. Wales has a poor economy, so touristizing slate mines is understandable. Dress warmly and don't miss the slate-splitting demonstration, open to all, at the end of the tramway tour (daily 10:00-18:00, closing at 17:00 in winter, two tours offered—the "deep mine" tour features the social life, the tramway focuses on the working life—£5 for one tour or £7.50 for both, tel. 01766/830523.)

Sleeping in Ruthin
(£1 = about $1.50, tel. code: 01824)

Sleep code: **S**=Single, **D**=Double/Twin, **T**=Triple, **Q**=Quad, **B**=Bath/Shower, **WC**=Toilet, **CC**=Credit Card (**V**isa, **M**astercard, **A**mex).

Bryn Awel—Beryl and John Jones run a warm, traditional, charming farmhouse B&B in the hamlet of Bontuchel just outside of Ruthin (D-£30, £32 for one-nighters, special 1995 price with this book, tel. 702481). Beryl is an excellent cook, and eager to help you with touring tips and a few key Welsh words. She can call and reserve the medieval banquet for you. From Ruthin, take the Bala road, #494, then the B5105 Cerrigydrudion Road. Turn right after the church, at the Bontuchel/Cyffylliog sign. Bryn Awel is on the right, 1½ miles down the little road. Go to the Bridge Hotel and backtrack 200 yards.

Eleanor Jones' B&B is in a cozy 15th-century Tudor home near the castle, town square, and bus stop. This place, with a library, grand piano, and royal breakfast, is a downtown gem (three huge rooms, £15.50 per person, 8a Castle Street, tel. 702748).

The Wine Vaults, run by Mrs. Taylor, is a musty old inn right on Ruthin's main square with a pub downstairs. This is the most central location possible, but less cozy than a B&B (four doubles or twins-£32, tel. 702067).

Eyarth Station, a well-run modern home in what used to be a train station, is set peacefully in the countryside a mile south of Ruthin (DB-£38, Llanfair D.C., LL15 2EE, tel. 703643, Jen and Albert Spencer).

Margaret Ranson's B&B, (DB-£32, Rhianfa, Ffordd Llanrhydd, Ruthin, Clwyd. LL15, 1PP, near hospital, a 10-minute walk from the castle, tel. 702971, entirely no smoking), in a big brick home, is friendly, comfortable, and moderately priced.

The **Ruthin Castle** is the ultimate in creaky Old World elegance for North Wales. But, at £85 per double, it's a serious splurge (tel. 702664).

For inexpensive dorm beds, you'll need to go to the **Llangollen youth hostel** (£8 per bed in 15-bed rooms, 15 miles from Ruthin, tel. 01978/860330).

Eating in Ruthin

The **Anchor Pub** is fairly expensive, with good food. The **Cross Keys Inn,** just west of town, is a friendly Ruthin pub serving excellent meals. Also consider the **Manor House Hotel Restaurant** for a moderate dinner. The **Chardonney's Wine Bar** offers good food and candlelit atmosphere and the **Eagles Pub** serves cheaper pub grub. The cafeteria in the crafts center next to the TI is bright and cheery. The **White Horse** pub, a mile out of town on the A525, serves good dinners.

Welsh

The Welsh language is alive and well. In a pub, impress your friends (or make some) by toasting the guy who might have just bought your drink. Say *Yeach-hid dah* (Good health to you) and *Dee olch* (thank you) or *Dee olch un vowr* (thanks very much). If the beer's bad, just make something up.

Transportation Connections

From Ironbridge Gorge, catch a bus to Telford (7 miles). At Telford, get on the Birmingham-Shrewsbury train (hrly, 60 min), transfer at Shrewsbury, and take the train to Wrexham (6/day, 40 min). Pick up a North Wales bus and train schedule at the station, and ask about Rover and Ranger passes. From Wrexham, catch a bus to Ruthin via Mold (hrly, 2 hrs).

Route Tips for Drivers

Ironbridge Gorge to Ruthin: Drive for an hour to Wales via A5 through Shrewsbury, crossing into Wales at the pretty castle town of Chirk. There, take A5 to Llangollen. Cross the bridge in Llangollen, turn left, and follow A542 and A525 past the romantic Valle Crucis Abbey, over the scenic Horseshoe Pass, and into Ruthin.

Ruthin to Caernarfon (56 miles) to Blaenau (34 miles) to Ruthin (35 miles): Every road in North Wales has its charm, but this day includes the best—lots of scenic wandering on small roads. From Ruthin, take B5105 (the steepest road off the main square) and follow the signs to Cerrigydrudion. Then follow A5 into Betws-y-Coed with a possible quick detour to the Trefriw Woolen Mill (3 miles north on B5106, well signposted). Continue west on A5 to Capel Curig, then take A4086 over the rugged Pass of Llanberis, just under the summit of Mt. Snowdon (to the south, behind those clouds), and on to Caernarfon. Park under the castle (very central) in the harborside car park.

Leaving Caernarfon, take the lovely A4085 southeast through Beddgelert to Penrhyndeudraeth. (Make things even more beautiful by taking the little B4410 road from Garreg through Rhyd.) Then take A487 toward Maentwrog, and A496 to Blaenau Ffestiniog. Go through the dark, depressing mining town of Blaenau Ffestiniog on A470 until you wind up in the hills of slate and turn right into the Llechwedd Slate Mine.

After the mine, A470 continues north on the most scenic stretch of all (past a ruined castle and several remote, intriguing B&Bs) through Dolwyddelan and back to A5. For a high and desolate detour, return to Ruthin via the windy, windy (curvy, blowy) A543 road over the stark moors to the Sportsman's Arms Pub (the highest pub in Wales, good food).

BLACKPOOL, ENGLAND'S CONEY ISLAND

This is Britain's fun puddle, where every Englishman goes but none will admit it. It's England's most-visited attraction, the private domain of its working class, and a favorite of kids of any age. When I told Brits I was Blackpool-bound, their expression soured and they asked, "Oh, God. Why?" Because it's the affordable escape of North England's Anne and Andy Capps. It's an ears-pierced-while-you-wait, tipsy-toupee kind of place. Tacky, yes. Low-brow, okay. But it's as English as can be, and that's what you're here for.

Spend the day "muckin' about" the beach promenade of fortune-tellers, fish-and-chips joints, amusement piers, warped mirrors, and Englanders wearing hats with built-in ponytails. A million greedy doors try every trick to get you inside. Huge arcade halls advertise free toilets and broadcast bingo numbers into the streets; the wind machine under a wax Marilyn Monroe blows at a steady gale; and the smell of fries, tobacco, and sugar is everywhere. Milk comes in raspberry or banana in this land where people under incredibly bad wigs look normal. If you're bored in Blackpool, you're just too classy.

Planning Your Time

Blackpool is easy by car or train. Ideally, get to Blackpool around lunchtime for a free afternoon and evening to make bubbles in this cultural mudpuddle. Speed demons with a car can treat it as a midday break (it's just off the M6) and continue north. If you have kids, they'll want more time here (it's cheaper than Disneyland). If you're before or beyond kids and not into kitsch and greasy spoons, skip it. If the weather's great and you love nature, the Lakes are just a few hours north. A visit to Blackpool does sharpen the wonders of Windermere.

Orientation (tel. code: 01253)

Everything clusters along the 6-mile beachfront promenade, a tacky, glittering strip-mall of fun. Each of the three amusement piers has its own personality: north—sedate, central—young fun, south—family (with a Wild West and circus theme). Jutting up near the north pier is Blackpool's stubby Eiffel-type tower.

Blackpool

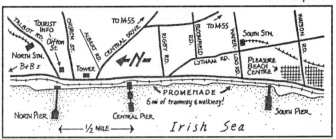

Tourist Information

Just north of Blackpool Tower, you'll find the TI (9:00-17:00, 10:00-16:00 on Sunday, shorter hours off-season, tel. 21623 or 26666 for 24-hour recorded entertainment information). Get the city map (35p), pick up brochures on the amusement centers, and ask about special shows.

Getting Around

Vintage trolley cars run up and down the waterfront, connecting all of the sights (70p a ride or £3.50 for a day-pass). The train station is just 3 blocks from the center.

Sights—Blackpool

▲**Blackpool Tower**—This vertical fun center celebrated its 100th birthday in 1994. You pay about £7 to get in; after that, the fun is free. Work your way up from the bottom through layer after layer of noisy entertainment: circus, bug zone, space world, dinosaur land, aquarium, and the silly house of horrors. Have a coffee break in the very elegant ballroom with barely live music and golden oldies dancing to golden oldies all day. The finale, at the tip of this 500-foot-tall symbol of Blackpool, is a smashing view, especially at sunset (daily 10:00-23:00).

▲▲**Variety Show**—Blackpool always has a few razzle-dazzle music, dancing-girl, racy-humor, magic, and tumbling shows. Box offices around town can give you a rundown on what's available (tickets, £5 to £12). I enjoy the "old-time music hall shows." The shows are corny—neither hip nor polished—but it's fascinating to be surrounded by hundreds of partying British seniors, swooning again and waving their hankies to the predictable beat. Busloads of happy widows come from all corners of North England to giggle at jokes I'd never tell my grandma.

The Illuminations—Blackpool was the first town in England to "go electric." Now, every September and October, Blackpool stretches its tourist season by illuminating its 6 miles of waterfront with countless lights, all blinking and twinkling, to the delight of those who visit this electronic festival. The American in me kept saying, "I've seen bigger and I've seen better," but I filled his mouth with cotton candy and just had some simple fun like everyone else on my specially decorated tram.

▲**Pleasure Beach**—These 42 acres littered with more than 80 rides (including "the best selection of white-knuckle rides in Europe"), ice-skating shows, cabarets, and amusements attract 6 million people a year. Its newest attraction: "the world's fastest and highest" roller coaster (235 feet, 85 mph). Admission is free, rides aren't (tel. 341033). There are several other major amusement centers, including a popular water-park called Sand Castle.

▲▲▲**People-Watching**—Blackpool's top sight is its people. You'll see England here like nowhere else. Grab someone's hand and a big stick of "rock" (candy) and stroll. Ponder the thought of actually retiring here to spend your last years, day after day, surrounded by Blackpool and wearing a hat with a built-in ponytail.

Sleeping in Blackpool
(£1 = about $1.50, tel. code: 01253)

Blackpool's 140,000 people provide 120,000 beds in 3,500 mostly dumpy, cheap, nondescript hotels and B&Bs. It's in the business of accommodating the English who can't afford to go to Spain. Almost all the B&Bs have the same design—minimal character, maximum number of springy beds—and charge £10 to £15 per person. If you arrive by midday, you should have no trouble finding a place. September to November and summer weekends are most crowded. My listings are on the waterfront. View rooms seem to be a bit bigger (and cost no more), but suffer from a little trolley noise. The first three are in the quiet area, about a mile or two north of the Tower, with easy parking and easy access to the center on the trolley. All B&Bs charge a little more during the Illuminations. Prices may be soft in off-season.

Sleep code: **S**=Single, **D**=Double/Twin, **T**=Triple, **Q**=Quad, **B**=Bath/Shower, **WC**=Toilet, **CC**=Credit Card (**V**isa, **M**astercard, **A**mex).

The Robin Hood Hotel is a super place, cheery, family-run, with a big, welcoming living room and 12 newly and tastefully refurbished rooms with the only sturdy beds I found. (£20 per person, £18 for 2-night stays, CC:VM, no smoking in bedrooms, 1½ miles north of Tower across from a peaceful stretch of beach, 100 Queens Promenade, North Shore FY2 9NS, tel. 351599, Pam and Colin Webster.)

The Sheralea, a few doors down, is also family-run, new-ish, clean and cheery (a bit pricey at D-£34, DB-£38, springy beds, one family room with a bunk and a double; 86 Queens Promenade, tel. 357694, Ruth and Brian Catlow).

The Prefect Hotel is all smiles and pink-flamingo pretty. (Divine would've loved it.) It's shabby but spacious-for-Blackpool with all the fun touches (S-£14, D-£28, DB-£32, 2 miles north of Tower at 204 Queens Promenade, FY2 9JS, tel. 352699, Bill and Pauline Acton).

The Belmont Private Hotel, right in the center, is not quite as terrible as its neighbors. Right on the waterfront, it's family-run with a decent meal service and a pleasant TV waterfront lounge (S-£15.50, D-£31, DB-£35, cheaper for 2 nights, springy beds; south of Tower between the central and south pier at 299 Promenade, Blackpool South, FY1 6AL, tel. 45815, Frank and Joan Linacre). Their son James swears (believably) he'll eat your breakfast if you show up one minute after 9:00. **The Holmhurst Hotel** (14 Reads Ave., tel. 325977, Carol and Chris Coureau) is also a decent value.

Train Connections

If you're heading to (or from) Blackpool by train, you'll usually transfer at Preston (4/hr, 30 min). To the **Lake District** you'll take the Preston-Penrith train (hrly, 1 hr) and catch a bus to Keswick (6/day, 40 min); **York** (hrly, 4½ hrs, change at Manchester). For points south (**Ironbridge Gorge, Cotswolds, Bath, North Wales**) you'll have several transfers but find fast and frequent trains. To **London** you'll change in Manchester (2/hr, 5 hrs).

Near Blackpool: Liverpool

Liverpool, a gritty but surprisingly enjoyable city, is a fascinating stop for Beatles fans and those who would like to look urban England straight in its problem-plagued eyes.

Tourist Info: Tel. 0151/709-3631. The bus and train stations are very central.

Train Connections, Liverpool to: Blackpool (hrly, 2 hrs, transfer at Preston), **York** (hrly, 3 hrs), **London** (hrly, 3 hrs).

Sights—Liverpool

Merseyside Maritime Museum—This interesting museum tells the story of this once-prosperous shipping center—ships, immigrations, hard times, and good times (£1.50, daily 10:30-17:30). Nearby are plenty of shops and restaurants.

The Beatles Story—An exhibition that tells the whole rockin' story (near the Maritime Museum, at Albert Dock, daily 10:00-18:00).

Matthew Street—Beatles fans will want to explore Matthew Street, including the famous, now-restored Cavern Club and the Beatles Shop at #31.

Museum of Liverpool Life—Get a good look at the workaday story of the town (next door to the Beatles Shop, on Matthew Street, daily 10:30-17:30).

Route Tips for Drivers

Ruthin to Liverpool: From Ruthin, get to the M53, which tunnels under the Mersey River. Once in Liverpool, follow signs to Pier Head and and Albert Dock where you'll find a huge free car park next to all the sights. Leaving Liverpool, drive north along the waterfront following signs to M58, then M6, and finally M55 into Blackpool.

Ruthin to Blackpool (100 miles): From Ruthin, take A494 through the town of Mold and follow the blue signs to the motorway. M56 zips you to M6, where you'll turn north toward Preston and Lancaster. After Preston, take M55 into Blackpool and drive as close as you can to the stubby Eiffel-type tower in the town center. Downtown parking is terrible. If you're not spending the day, head for one of the huge £6/day garages. If you're spending the night, drive to the waterfront and head north. My top B&Bs are north on the Promenade (easy parking).

LAKE DISTRICT

In the pristine Lake District, Wordsworth's poems still shiver in trees and
ripple on ponds. This is a land where
nature rules and man keeps a wide-eyed but
low profile. Relax, recharge, take a cruise or a
hike, maybe even write a poem. Renew your poetic license
at Wordsworth's famous Dove Cottage.

The Lake District, about 30 by 30 miles, is nature's
lush, green playground. Explore it by foot, bike, bus, or car.
The sky will cloud and clear. You'll probably have rain
mixed with brilliant bright spells. Handy pubs offer atmospheric shelter at every turn.

The most impressive sights and hikes cluster around
the most beautiful lakes in the district: Derwentwater,
Windermere, and Ullswater. The handiest home base for
the Lake District, especially if you're relying on public
transportation, is Keswick.

Planning Your Time

If great scenery is commonplace in your life, the Lake
District can be more soothing (and rainy) than exciting. To
save time, you could easily make this area a one-night
stand—or even a quick drive-through.

With a car and a three-week trip in Britain, I'd spend
the better part of two days and two nights in the area. Arrive
by late morning, drive along Windermere, tour Dove
Cottage, and get to Glenridding on Ullswater in time for the
14:00 boat. Hike 6 miles (14:30-18:00) from Howtown back
to Glenridding. Drive to your farmhouse B&B near Keswick.

On your second day: Explore Buttermere Lake, drive
over Honister Pass, explore Derwentwater (from Keswick
cruise to High Brandlehow Pier, hike up to Cat Bells and
down to Hawes End Pier, catch boat back to Keswick).
Evening at same B&B.

Those without a car will use Keswick as a springboard.
Cruise the lake and hike in Cat Bells area. Consider minibus
excursions from Keswick. If you need a vacation from your
vacation, use this day to just vegetate and recharge.

Keswick (tel. code: 017687)

As far as touristy lake-district centers go, Keswick is an enjoyable town (population: 5,000). This is your logistical headquarters with everything you need, including plenty of good B&Bs and an easy bus connection to the nearest train station at Penrith, as well as several mediocre but entertaining museums and a suburb called Barf.

Keswick is situated right on the best single lake in the area for our visit, Derwentwater. Keswick's market square, TI office, recommended B&Bs, bike rental shop, bus station, Mountain Goat minibus tour starting point, lakeside boat dock, and a central car park are all within a 5-minute walk of each other.

Tourist Info: The TI has local and regional info, at Market Square (tel. 017687/72645).

Getting Around the Lake District

A short visit without wheels is pretty easy, particularly if you keep it simple and focus only on the best, Keswick and Derwentwater.

Hiking: Take advantage of several publications (from the TI or in most B&B libraries), especially *Explore Lakeland and Cumbria: Out and About From Keswick* (which details the best hikes from Keswick, taking advantage of one-way bus connections) and *15 Walks From Keswick* (£2). Consider buying a guidebook, the Ordnance Survey *Lake District Tourist Map* (£3), or possibly the more focused 1:25,000 *OS Outdoor Leisure* map for the northwest quarter of the area. This lush world is not as gentle as it looks. Every year, careless hikers underestimate the need for rain gear, sturdy shoes, and maps. Get specific hiking advice from one of the many Tourist Information Centres that dot the district. Each is especially knowledgeable for its specific locality. For the latest north lakes weather report, call 017687/72803.

Biking: A bike rental shop is near the Keswick TI.

By Bus: Pick up a schedule at the Keswick bus station. If your time is limited, try a bus tour. Mountain Goat Tours run all-day (£20) and half-day (£10) minibus tours daily in summer from Keswick. They are rugged, informative (led by established mountain guides), and great for people who'd like to see the area without hiking and without wheels.

Lake District

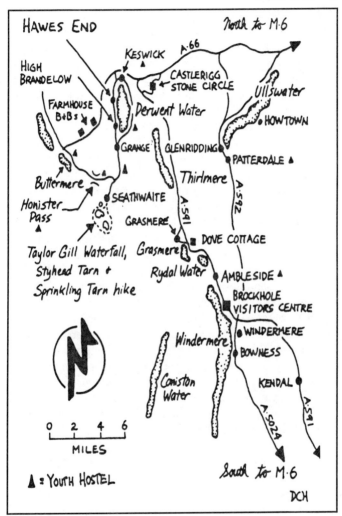

Unfortunately, you may not know if your tour will reach its
minimum number of six passengers until shortly before departure (office at Keswick central car park, tel. 73962).
By Car: Nothing is far from Keswick and Derwentwater. Get
a good map, get off the big roads, and leave the car, at least
occasionally, for some walking. In the summer, the Keswick-
Ambleside-Windermere-Bowness area suffers from congestion.

Sights—Derwentwater Area

▲▲**Derwentwater**—This is one of the region's most photographed and popular lakes. With four islands, good circular boat service, plenty of trails, and the pleasant town of Keswick at its north end, Derwentwater entertains.

The roadside views aren't much, so walk or cruise. You can walk around the lake (fine trail, but floods in heavy rains, 9 miles, 3 hrs), cruise it (50 min), or do a hike/sail mix. I suggest a hike/sail trip around the lake. Boats run about every 30 minutes in each direction and make seven stops on each 50-minute round-trip. The best hour-long lakeside walk is between the docks at High Brandlehow and Hawse End. The boat trip costs £4.40 per circle with free stop-overs, or 70p per segment. Stand on the pier or the boat may not stop.

▲▲**Cat Bells High Ridge Hike**—For a great "king of the mountain" feeling, great all-around views, and a close-up look at the weather blowing over the ridge, hike about 2 hours from Hawse End up along the ridge to Cat Bells (1,480 feet), and down to High Brandlehow. From there you can catch the boat, or take the easy path along the shore of Derwentwater to your Hawes End starting point. This is probably the most dramatic family walk in the area. For a longer and higher hike, continue farther along the ridge to Black Crag, and walk down to Grange or High Brandlehow. There's a not-particularly-safe little car park at Hawes End. From Keswick, the lake, or your farmhouse B&B, you can see silhouetted stick figures hiking along this ridge.

▲▲▲**A Waterfall and Two Tarns Hike**—For a more difficult and equally rewarding 3-hour Derwentwater-area hike, park south of Borrowdale, at the end of the long dead-end road to Seathwaite. Go through the farm, cross the river, continue along the river (it's difficult to follow the trail; stay near the river) and up a steep, rocky climb to the Taylor Gill Force, a 140-foot waterfall. There's a tough hundred yards of rocky scramble, but the trail improves at the falls. Keep walking to two sleeping-beauty tarns (bodies of water too small to be lakes, Styhead and Sprinkling Tarn), circle the Seathwaite Fell to Stockley Bridge, and follow the bridle-path back to your car. For an easier version, just hike to the first tarn and backtrack, eventually taking a right turn leading to Stockley Bridge (get specifics on this hike from the TI).

▲▲**Buttermere**—This ideal little lake with a lovely encircling 4-mile stroll offers non-stop, no-sweat, lakeland beauty. If you're not a hiker but kind of wish you were, take this walk. If you're very short on time, at least stop here and get your shoes dirty. (Parking and pubs in Buttermere village.) A great road over the rugged Honister Pass, strewn with nosy ragamuffin goats and glacial debris, connects Buttermere with Borrowdale and Derwentwater.

▲▲**Castlerigg Stone Circle**—These 38 stones, 90 feet across, 3,000 years old, are mysteriously laid out on a line between the two tallest peaks on the horizon. For maximum goosebumps, be here at sunrise or sunset (free, open all the time, just east of Keswick, follow brown signs, 3 minutes off A66, easy parking).

Hard Knott Pass—Only 1,300 feet above sea level, this pass is a thriller, with a narrow, winding, steeply graded road. Just over the pass are the scant, but evocative, remains of the Hard Knott Roman Fortress. Great views, miserable rainstorms, frustrating and very slow when the one-lane road with turn-outs is clogged by traffic.

Sights—Windermere Area

▲▲**Brockhole National Park Visitors Centre**—Check the events board as you enter. The center offers a 17-minute introduction-to-the-lakes slide show (call for times), an information desk, organized walks, exhibits, a bookshop, a good cafeteria, gardens, nature walks, and a large car park. It's in a stately old lakeside mansion between Ambleside and the town of Windermere on A591 (daily 10:00-17:00 April-October, free entry but £2.20 to park, tel. 015394/46601). The bookshop has an excellent selection of maps and guidebooks. I enjoyed the refreshingly opinionated *Good Guide to the Lakes* by Hunter Davies (£5).

▲▲**Dove Cottage**—Wordsworth, the poet whose appreciation of nature and back-to-basics lifestyle put this area on the map, spent his most productive years (1799-1808) in this well-preserved old cottage on the edge of Grasmere. Today it's the obligatory sight for any Lake District visit. Even if you're not a fan, Wordsworth's "plain living and high thinking," his appreciation of nature, his romanticism, and the ways his friends unleashed their creative talents are very appealing. The cottage tour and adjoining museum are excellent. Even a speedy, jaded museum-goer will want at least an hour here (£4, daily 9:30-17:30, tel. 015394/35544).

Rydal Mount—Wordsworth's final, higher-class home with a lovely garden and view lacks the charm of Dove Cottage. Just down the road from Dove Cottage, it's worthwhile only for Wordsworth fans.

▲**Beatrix Potter Sights**—Many come to the lakes on a Beatrix Potter pilgrimage. Sensing that, entrepreneurial locals have dreamed up a number of BP sights. It can be confusing. Most important (and least advertised) is Hill Top Farm, the 17th-century cottage where she wrote many of her Peter Rabbit books (£3.30, April-October 11:00-17:00, closed Thursday and Friday, next to Sawrey, near Hawkshead, tel. 015394/36269). Small, dark, and crowded, it gives a good look at her life and work. (The nearby village of Hawkshead and the short walk to the tiny lake, Tarn Hows, are both worth a stop.) The Beatrix Potter Gallery shows off BP's original drawings and watercolor illustrations used in her children's storybooks, and tells more about her life and work (£2.50, closed Saturday and Sunday, on Main Street in Hawkshead, tel. 015394/36355). *The World of Beatrix Potter*, a high-tech film and video tour into the world of Mrs. Tiggywinkle and company, is a hit with families and the Japanese (£2.75, daily 10:00-19:00, in Bowness near Windermere town, tel. 015394/88444). And up in the north, Keswick has gotten in on the BP action with a Beatrix Potter's Lake District exhibit, little more than a 16-minute National Trust video effort to remind us that BP was an environmentalist and we should be, too (not worth £2.50, daily 10:00-17:00, tel. 017687/75173).

Sights—Ullswater Area

▲▲▲**Ullswater Hike and Boat Ride**—Long narrow Ullswater, with 8 miles of diverse and grand Lake District scenery, is considered by many to be the most beautiful lake in the area. While you can drive it or cruise it, I'd ride the boat from the south tip halfway up and hike back. Start at the Glenridding dock. Boats leave Glenridding regularly from 10:00 to 16:30, 17:45 in July and August. (Afternoon departures at 14:00 and 14:40, get there a little early in summer, 35-minute ride, £2.50, tel. 017684/82229). Ride to the first stop, Howtown, halfway up the lake. Then spend 4 hours hiking and dawdling along the well-marked path by the lake south to Patterdale and then along the road back to Glenridding. This is a serious 6-mile walk with good views, varied terrain, and a few bridges and farms along the way. Wear good shoes and be prepared for rain. For a shorter hike, consider a circular walk from Howtown Pier. (Round-trip boat rides cost only 60p more than one-way.) There are several steamer trips daily up and down Ullswater. A good rainy-day plan is to ride the covered boat up and down the 8-mile lake (2 hrs) or to Howtown and back (1 hr). Novice pony-trekkers can rent a pony at the Side Farm for a £6.50, hour-long scenic clip-clop above the lake (afternoon rides, tougher 2- and 4-hour rides too, near Patterdale, tel. 017684/82337).

Helvellyn—Often considered the best high-mountain hike in the Lake District, this dangerous, breathtaking, round-trip hike from Glenridding has a glorious ridge-walk finale. Be careful, do this 4-hour hike only in good weather, and get advice from the Glenridding tourist office. The views are stupendous, but keep one eye on the trail.

Sleeping in and near Keswick
(£1 = about $1.50, tel. code: 017687)

The Lake District abounds with attractive B&Bs, guest houses, and youth hostels. It needs them all when summer hordes threaten the serenity of this romantics' mecca. The region is most crowded on Sundays and in July and August. Saturdays (when people's week-long visits end) are not bad. With the mobility of a car, you should have no trouble finding a room. But to get a particular place, it's best to call ahead. Those using public transportation should stay in Keswick (first five listings). With a car, drive into a remote farmhouse experience (later listings). Those on a tight budget should take advantage of the area's fine youth hostels (listed last).

Sleep code: **S**=Single, **D**=Double/Twin, **T**=Triple, **Q**=Quad, **B**=Bath/Shower, **WC**=Toilet, **CC**=Credit Card (Visa, Mastercard, Amex).

Berkeley Guest House, a big slate mansion on a quiet, elegant crescent between the bus station, the town, and the lakeside park, rubs drainpipes with fancier places. Enthusiastically run by Barbara Crompton, it has a pleasant lounge, cramped hallways, and thoughtfully appointed, comfortable rooms. Request a view room. The chirpy but simple twin in the attic is a fine value if you don't mind the stairs (D-£29 to £31, DB-£37 to £39; The Heads, Keswick, Cumbria, CA12 5ER, tel. 74222).

The **Highfield Hotel**, next door, is good for those wanting the impersonality of a classy hotel with better public areas than rooms (S-£17, DB-£45, DB with big bay-window lake views-£55; The Heads, tel. 72508).

Abacourt House, an old Victorian townhouse completely re-done by Sheila and Bill Newman, is on a quiet street lined with mostly dumpy B&Bs 2 blocks from the bus station and the town center. This non-smoking place is small but clean and cheery, with a dark woody feeling and an interesting library. All four doubles have firm beds, TVs, and shiny modern bathrooms (DB-£40; 26 Stanger Street, Keswick, CA12 5JU, tel. 72967).

The **Rowan Tree**, another small, cheery, smoke-free place, a few doors down the street, has a few rooms without private facilities, making it less expensive and a fine budget value (D-£28, DB-£36; 18 Stanger Street, tel. 74304, Liz and Dave Thompson).

Ridgeway Guest House, on the top of the street, is a bit smoky and musty, but has decent beds and is just plain cheap (S-£12, D-£24; 25 Stanger Street, tel. 72582, Mrs. Hodgson).

Birkrigg Farm is the perfect farmhouse B&B. Mrs. Margaret Beaty offers visitors a comfy lounge, evening tea (good for socializing with her other guests), a classy breakfast, territorial view, perfect peace, and, upon request, a hot-water bottle to warm up your bed (traditionally, farmhouses lacked central heating). Her 220-acre working farm, shown on the Ordnance Survey map, is on a tiny road halfway between Braithwaite and Buttermere in the vast, majestic Newlands Valley. Leave Keswick heading west on the Cockermouth road (A66). Take the Newlands Valley exit and follow signs through Newlands Valley (direction: Buttermere) for a couple of miles until you see the B&B sign (£14-£15 per person in S, D, T, or Q, family deals, one shared shower for six rooms, open March-November; Birkrigg Farm, Newlands Pass Rd., Keswick, Cumbria, CA12 5TS, tel. 78278).

Keskadale Farm B&B is another great farmhouse experience with valley views and flapjack hospitality. This is a working farm with lots of curly-horned sheep and three rooms to rent (£14.50-£15 per person in D or T, March-November, 2 minutes farther down Newlands Pass Road near a hairpin turn, Keskadale Farm, Newlands, Keswick CA12 5TS, tel. 78544, Margaret Harryman).

Since neither farmhouse serves dinner, take the lovely 10-minute drive to Buttermere for your evening meal at the **Fish Hotel** pub (£5, 18:00-21:00 nightly, limited menu, good fish, chips for vegetables) or the **Bridge Hotel** pub (£6 or £7, 18:00-21:30 nightly, more interesting menu and crowd).

For village B&Bs south of Derwentwater, try the beautiful Valley of Borrowdale. The tidy village of Grange has several neatly stacked slate B&Bs. The smaller stone-farm, mossy-roofed, cobbled village jumble of Rosthwaite is cow-dung basic. The Tolkienesque **Yew Tree Farm** (DB-£36, tel. 77675, Hazel Relph) and the less ancient, more spacious **Nook Farm** (D-£28, DB-£36, tel. 77677, Carole Jackson) are each comfortable but hearthocentric, with very old, sagging floors; thick, whitewashed walls; three rooms and small doorways. If you're under 6 feet tall and interested in farm noises and the Old World, these are for you.

Youth Hostels

The Lake District has 30 youth hostels and needs more. Most are in great old buildings, handy sources of information, fun socially, and inexpensive (£6-£9 a bed). In the summer, you'll need to call ahead. For this plan, consider the Buttermere **King George VI Memorial Hostel**, a quarter-mile south of Buttermere village on Honister Pass Road (good food, family rooms, royal setting, tel. 70245), or the **Longthwaite Hostel**, secluded in Borrowdale Valley just south of Rosthwaite (well-run, drying rooms, tel. 77257). Two former hotels now operate as hostels: **Keswick** (center of town, tel. 72484) and **Derwentwater** (2 miles south of Keswick, tel. 77246).

Transportation Connections

The nearest train station to Keswick is in Penrith, on a
major rail line running north and south. The X5 Lakes Link
buses connect **Penrith** and Keswick (6/day, 8:35-18:20,
3/Sunday, 40 min, £2.50, tel. 01946/63222).

Trains from Penrith to: Oban (hrly to Glasgow in 2 hrs,
then to Oban—3/day, 3 hrs), **Edinburgh** (5/day, 2 hrs),
Blackpool (hrly to Preston in 1½ hrs, transfer to Blackpool—hrly, 30 min), and **York** (one bus a day to Keswick,
4 hrs).

Route Tips for Drivers

Blackpool to Windermere (60 miles, 2 hrs): Drivers leave
Blackpool taking M55 south to M6. Then zip north on M6.
Exit on A590/A591 through the towns of Kendal and
Windermere to reach Brockhole National Park Visitors
Centre. From Brockhole, take the tiny road northeast
directly to Troutbeck. Then follow A592 to Glenridding
and lovely Ullswater. Just before Glenridding, turn right into
the car park and boat dock (get a self-service pay 'n' display
parking sticker). Catch the 14:00 boat, sail for 35 minutes,
get off at Howtown, and hike back to your car. Then drive
north along the lake, turning left on A5091 and left again on
A66 to Keswick. Your B&B is over Newlands Pass.

For the drive north to **Oban**, see the Highlands chapter.

YORK

Historical York has world-class sights and a past that won't quit. Marvel at York's Minster, the finest Gothic church in England, and ramble through the Shambles, York's wonderfully preserved medieval quarter. Enjoy a walking tour led by an old Yorker. Hop a train at Europe's greatest Railway Museum, travel to the 1800s in the York Castle Museum, and head back to the year 994 at Jorvik, the original Viking settlement.

Planning Your Time

York is a great sightseeing city. On a three-week trip through Britain, it deserves two nights and a day. To maximize sightseeing time, catch the city walking tour at 19:00 on the evening of your arrival. The next morning you might walk the medieval wall to the Castle Museum. This museum is actually worth three hours. Have a touristy walk through the Shambles, browse the Newgate Market, lunch in the Golden Fleece pub if you're in the mood for some second-hand smoke. Tour the Minster at 16:00 before catching the 17:00 evensong service. Wander down to the Jorvik exhibit just before it closes at 19:00 to see it without the wait. Still more energy? Take the Ghost walk. This schedule assumes you're there in the summer (evening orientation walk) and that there's an evensong on. Confirm plans with TI first. Major omission/alternate: the National Railway Museum.

Orientation (tel. code: 01904)

York is big only in historical terms. Virtually everything—the sights, train station, tourist information, and B&Bs—is within a few minutes' walk. The farthest walk a visitor would make (from B&B across the old town to the Castle Museum) takes no more than 15 minutes.

Bootham Bar, a gate in the medieval town wall, is the hub of your York visit. At Bootham Bar (and on Exhibition Square facing it), you'll find the TI, the starting points for most walking tours and bus tours, and handy access to the medieval town wall, and Gillygate, lined with good eateries.

Tourist Information

The TI at Bootham Bar has a free *What's On* and can sell
you a map and answer your questions (Monday-Saturday
9:00 -19:00, Sunday 10:00-13:00 in July and August,
Monday-Saturday 9:00-17:00, closed Sunday the rest of the
year, tel. 01904/621756). It sells a £1 "discount card" which
gives two adults and two kids substantial discounts on major
sights. If a single traveler uses it twice it's worthwhile.

Trains

The station is a 5-minute walk from town (turn left down
station Road and follow the crowd toward the gothic towers
of the minster which you'll see in the distance. After the
bridge a block before the minster, signs to the TI will send
you left.

While no one seems to use them, buses #30, #31, and
#32 go from the station to my recommended B&Bs.
Otherwise it's a £2.30 taxi ride.

In York, a "bar" is a gate and a "gate" is a street (from
the Norse, a reminder of the town's Viking heritage).

Sights—York

▲▲▲**Walking Tours**—Charming local volunteer guides
give energetic and entertaining free 2-hour walks through
York (daily, 10:15 and 14:15 April-October, plus 19:00 June-
August, leaving from the TI). These are better than the
gimmicky commercial walks. There are many other York
walking tours. The Ghost tours, offered after nightfall, are
popular (but the evening free walks also throw in a few ghosts).
For a walkman tour you can rent one of three entertaining
"Yorspeed" audio tours ("The Streets," around "The Walls,"
or with "The Ghosts," 1 hour each without stops, £4 for one,
£6 for two with this book, tel. 652653, from the TI).
▲**Guide Friday Hop-on and Hop-off Bus Tours**—York's
Guide Friday offers tour guides on speed who can talk
enthusiastically to three sleeping tourists in a gale on a topless double-decker bus for an hour without stopping. Buses
make the hour-long circuit, covering much that the city
walking tours don't (£5.50 for all day, departures every 10
or 15 minutes from 9:20 until around 18:00, tel. 640896).
While you can hop on and off where you like, the York

York

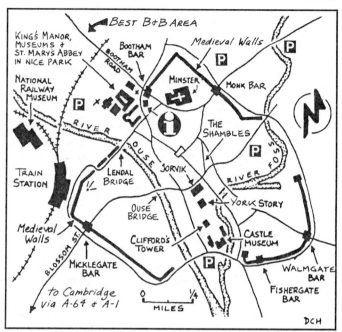

route is of no value from a transportation-to-the-sights point of view. I'd catch it at the TI and ride it all the way around or get off at the Railway Museum, skipping the last 5 minutes.

▲**City Walls**—The historic walls of York provide a fine 2-mile walk. Be sure to walk from Bootham Bar (gate) to Monk Bar for outstanding cathedral views. Open until dusk and free.

▲▲**The National Railway Museum**—This thunderous museum shows 150 fascinating years of British railroad history. Fanning out from a grand roundhouse are an array of historic cars and engines, including Queen Victoria's lavish royal car and the very first "stagecoaches on rails." There's much more, including exhibits on dining cars, post cars, Pullman cars, train posters, and videos. This is the biggest and best railroad museum anywhere (£4.20, Monday-Saturday 10:00-18:00, Sunday 11:00-18:00, tel. 621261).

▲▲▲**The York Minster (cathedral)**—The pride of York, this largest Gothic church in Britain is a brilliant example of how the High Middle Ages were far from dark. Pick up the *Welcome to the York Minster* flyer at the information desk and ask about a free guided tour. The helpful blue-armbanded Minster Guides are there to answer your questions. The east window is the largest medieval glass window in existence. For most, the chapter room and the crypt are not worth the admission. But the tower (£2, long climb, great view) and the undercroft/treasury (£1.80) are. The undercroft gives you a chance to climb down, archaeologically and physically, through the centuries to see the roots of the much smaller but still huge Norman church (Romanesque, 1100) which stood on this spot, and below that, to the Roman excavations. Constantine was proclaimed Roman emperor here in 306 A.D. The under-croft also give you a look at the modern concrete save-the-church foundations. The cathedral is open daily, 7:30-20:30 (tel. 624426). The chapter room, tower, and undercroft have shorter hours, usually 10:00-17:00. Evensong is a glorious chance to experience the cathedral in musical and spiritual action. Evensong services are held daily at 17:00. (16:00 on Saturday and Sunday, but usually spoken on Wednesday and when the choir is off). While a donation of £1.50 is reason-ably requested, if I'm visiting the undercroft or climbing the tower, I give it (and more) in the form of those admissions.

▲**The Shambles**—This is the most colorful old York street in the half-timbered core of town. Ye olde downtown York is very touristy but a window-shopping, people-watcher's delight. Wander through the Newgate Market a block over. The center of York is nearly traffic-free and a busker-filled joy for walking.

▲▲▲**York Castle Museum**—Truly one of Europe's top museums, this is a walk with Dickens, the closest thing to a time-tunnel experience England has to offer. It includes a magnificent collection of old shops well-stocked exactly as they were 150 years ago, costumes, armor, an incredible Anglo-Saxon helmet (from 750 A.D.), and the "every home needs one" exhibit showing the evolution of vacuum clean-ers, toilets, TVs, bicycles, stoves, and so on, from their crude beginnings to now. (£4, 9:30-18:00, Sunday 10:00-18:00, cafeteria, shop, car park; the £2 guidebook is unnecessary, but a nice souvenir, tel. 653611.)

▲▲**Jorvik**—The innovative museum of Viking York takes you back a thousand years—literally backward—in a little Disney-type train car. Then, still seated, you cruise slowly

for 13 minutes through the sounds, sights, and even smells of
the re-created Viking village of Jorvik. Next your little train
takes you through the actual excavation sight (best Viking
dig I've seen anywhere), then lets you off to browse through
a gallery of Viking shoes, combs, locks, and other intimate
glimpses of that redheaded culture (£4; daily 9:00-19:00;
November-March 9:00-17:30; tel. 643211). Don't be pres-
sured into buying the colorful guidebook with your ticket.
To minimize time in line—which can be more than an
hour—go very early (at 8:45) or very late. In summer the last
entrance is 19:00. Day-trippers make summer midday lines
routinely 2 hours long. Jorvik is not worth even a 30-minute
wait. Get there at 18:00 and you'll sail right in. Some love
this "ride"; others call it a gimmicky rip-off. While it has
inspired a chain of copycat historical rides around England,
most of which are also gimmicky rip-offs, I like Jorvik.
Honorable Mention—York has a number of other sights
and activities (described in TI material) which pale in com-
parison to the biggies but are worth a look if you have the
time. The York Story (£1.60, associated with, across the
street from, and pushed by the Castle Museum) is an exhibit
displaying the city's past, with a 45-minute video on the
history of York. It's good, straight history.

Sleeping in York
(£1 = about $1.50, tel. code: 01904)

I've listed peak-season book-direct prices. If you use the TI,
they'll charge you more. Outside of the peak July-August
months, York B&B prices get soft and some places may drop
by several pounds. Ask for off-season deals. I've limited my
recommendations to the handiest B&B neighborhood, just
outside the old town wall's Bootham gate, along the road
called Bootham. All are within about 5 minutes' walk of the
Minster and TI and a 10-minute or £2.30 taxi ride from the
station. If you're driving, take A19 into town. It becomes
Bootham and you'll find the B&Bs just before Bootham hits
York's medieval town gate.

These B&Bs are small, family-run, will generally hold a
room with a phone call, work hard to help their guests sightsee and eat smartly, have lots of fairly steep stairs, and are all
on quiet, residential side streets. Parking is generally no

York, Our Neighborhood

problem. Most places have their own spots or loaner permits for street parking. The train tracks bordering many places are used by the little Scarborough train that doesn't run at night.

Sleep code: **S**=Single, **D**=Double/Twin, **T**=Triple, **Q**=Quad, **B**=Bath/Shower, **WC**=Toilet, **CC**=Credit Card (**V**isa, **M**astercard, **A**mex).

Airden House—Susan and Keith Burrows keep this snug and traditional place simple and friendly. They are a great source of local travel tips. Airden House, the most central of these Bootham-area listings, has eight rooms, a grandfather-clock-cozy TV lounge, and brightness and warmth throughout. Two of their *en suite* doubles are way up on top (D-£36, DB-£40; 1 St. Mary's, York Y03 7DD, tel. 638915).

The Sycamore, run by Margaret and David Tyce, is a fine value with cozy rooms and plenty of personal touches, at the end of a dead-end right across from a fun-to-watch bowling green (D-£30, DB-£36, family deals, no lounge but TVs in the rooms; 19 Sycamore Place off Bootham Terrace, YO3 7DW, tel. 624712).

Astoria Hotel—Mr. and Mrs. Bradley offer 17 rooms in an old, well-worn, but respectable place (S-£16, SB-£16, D-£30, DB-£35, family deals, CC:V; 6 Grosvenor Terrace, Bootham, York, Y03 7AG, tel. 659558).

Claremont Guest House is a friendly, non-smoking house offering three rooms, thoughtful touches, and solid beds (D-£30, DB-£40; 18 Claremont Terrace off Gillygate, YO3 7EJ, tel. 625158, Gill and Martyn Cornell).

The Hazelwood is my most hotelesque listing. Ian and Carolyn McNabb run this elegant and spacious old 16-room place in a stately, proper way, paying careful attention to details and serving a classy breakfast (S-£22.50, D-£40, DWC-£41, DBWC-£48, DBWC with four-poster-£53, family deals, CC:VM, non-smoking, 1 ground-floor room, reserve by letter; 24 Portland St, Gillygate, YO3 7EH, tel. 626548, fax 628032).

White Doves is a cheery little place with four bright and comfy rooms (DB-£38, 20 Claremont Terrace off Gillygate, YO3 7EJ, tel. 625957, Pauline Pearce).

23 St. Mary's is a rococo riot. Mrs. Hudson has done everything super-correctly, and offers nine rooms with strong beds, modern facilities, a classy lounge and all the doily touches (SB-£30, DB-£56, no smoking; 23 St. Mary's, YO3 7DD, tel. 622738).

Queen Anne's Guest House is compact, clean, and cheery (D-£28, DB-£30 promised through 1995 with this book; 24 Queen Anne's Road, tel. 629389, Judy and David West). For similar prices, you could try **Arron Guest House** (42 Bootham Crescent, tel. 625927). **St. Mary's Hotel** is a decent non-smoking place (D-£32, DB-£44 with book through 1995, CC:V; 17 Longfield Terrace, tel. 626972, Barry Lyons).

The Golden Fleece—For a funky, murky, creaky experience right in the center of the old town, consider this historic 400-year-old pub that rents five rooms upstairs (pub closed at 23:00). The floors aren't level, the beds are four-posters, and the local crowd fills the ground-floor pub with smoke and belly laughs (D-£37, family room with a four-poster and bunks, 1-person jacuzzi in the shared bathroom, private car park; at the bottom end of the Shambles, 16 Pavement, York, YO1 2ND, tel. 625171).

York's Youth Hotel is clean, cheery, and well-run, with lots of extras like a kitchen, laundromat, games, and bar. They take no telephone reservations, but normally have beds until noon (D-£24, £11 in 4- to 6-bed dorms, sheets and breakfast extra, 11 Bishophill Senior Road, York YO1 1EF, tel. 625904 or 630613).

Eating in York

Good Meals Downtown

The old center is slathered with cute eateries. Consider one of several places along the street called Pavement. The **Golden Fleece** pub is a hopping place serving famous Yorkshire Pudding and hearty meals until 22:00. Next door, the **York Pie Shop** does traditional meat pies well. **Kites**, closer to the center, on Grape Lane, serves tasty, fresh, and unusual French and English meals at good prices. **Ye Olde Starre Inn**, the oldest pub in town, has yet to learn the art of cooking.

York is famous for its elegant teahouses. Around four-ish, drop into one for tea and cakes. **Betty's** is most famous, with people lining up to get in, but several others can satisfy your king- or queen-for-a-day desires.

Eating near Bootham Bar and Your B&B

For pub dinners, consider the **Coach House** (18:30-21:30 nightly, 20 Marygate, tel. 652780), **Elliot's Hotel Restaurant and Pub** (dinners nightly, just off Bootham Terrace), or one of several pubs on Gillygate. **Bootham Bistro** (18 Bootham, tel. 630678) is a cheery little no-smoking place serving good English meals for £5. Gillygate, which starts at Bootham Bar, is lined with interesting, cheap, healthy and/or fun eateries: **Mama Mia's** (#20 Gillygate, daily 11:30-14:00 and 17:30-23:00) is great for Italian. A popular extremely vegetarian place, **Miller's Yard Cafe**, is across the street and the **Phoenix** cooks first-class Chinese (eat-in or take-out). There's also a traditional little "chippie" (fish-and-chips joint) at #59 where tattooed people eat in and house-bound mothers take out. Or go with the latest pub-grub advice from the people who run your B&B.

For a reasonable, historic, handy lunch, try the **King's Manor Refectory** on Exhibition Square (through the court-yard on the left, lunch, noon-14:00, Monday-Friday). The tea room at the **Bootham Bar Hotel** (10:00-17:30 daily, 4 High Petergate, near the TI) serves a tasty and reasonable lunch.

Train Connections

York is on the speedy London-Edinburgh rail line. Trains go to: **Durham** (hrly, 1 hr) or **Edinburgh** (hrly, 3 hrs), **London** (hrly, 2 hrs, £44), **Bath** (via Bristol, hrly, 5 hrs), **Cambridge** (nearly hrly, 2 hrs with a change in Petersborough).

Near York: North York Moors

The North York Moors are a vacant lot compared with the Windermere Lakes District. But that's unfair competition. In the lonesome North York Moors, you can wander through the stark beauty of its time-passed villages, bored sheep, and powerful landscapes. Here are the highlights:

Sights—North York Moors

▲**The Moors**—Danby Lodge, the North York Moors Visitors Centre, provides the best orientation for exploring the moors. It's a grand old lodge offering exhibits, shows, and nature walks, an information desk with plenty of books and maps, brass-rubbing, a cheery cafeteria, and brochures on several good walks that start right there (free, daily 10:00-17:00, April-October, tel. 01287/660654).

North Yorkshire Moors Railway—If you're tired of driving (or without wheels), this 18-mile, 50-minute steam-engine ride from Grosmont and Goathland to Pickering goes through some of the best parts of the moors almost hourly. Unfortunately, the windows are small and dirty (wipe off the outside of yours before you roll), and the tracks are in a scenic gully (£10, tel. 01751/72508). Pickering, with its rural-life museum, castle, and Monday market, is worth a stop.

▲**Hutton-le-Hole**—This postcard-pretty town is home of the fine little Ryedale Museum, which illustrates "farm life in the moors" through reconstructed and furnished 18th-century local buildings (daily 10:30-17:30, April-October, tel. 017515/367). Car park and public toilets are nearby.

Castle Howard—Especially popular since the filming of "Brideshead Revisited," this is a fine palatial home but about half as interesting as Cotswolds' Blenheim Palace (late March-October, 2 buses a day from York, 30 minutes).

Rievaulx Abbey—A highlight of the North York Moors, but if you've seen other fine old abbeys, this is a rerun.

Staithes and Whitby—See Durham/North England chapter.

DURHAM AND NORTHEAST ENGLAND

Some of England's best history is harbored in the northeast. Hadrian's Wall reminds us that Britain was an important Roman colony 2,000 years ago. After a Roman ramble you can go to Holy Island where Christianity gained its first toehold in Britain. The logical next stop is Durham, to marvel at England's greatest Norman church and enjoy an evensong service. And, for a trip into the less distant past, spend a morning in the year 1900 at the Beamish Open-Air Folk Museum.

Planning Your Time

Of the sights described in this destination, only Durham and Hadrian's Wall are worth a stop on a three-week British train trip. By car you'll be driving right by Holy Island, Bamburgh, and the Beamish Folk Museum, so they're worth considering. Whitby and Staithes are seaside escapes worth a stop only for their escape value. Whitby is accessible by train but Staithes is for drivers.

By train, Durham is easy and worth at least a 3-hour stop. Hadrian's Wall is a headache without a car and, while certainly do-able by public transportation, probably not worth the trouble on a rushed train trip.

By car I'd connect Edinburgh and York by this string of sights, spending a night on Hadrian's Wall and a night in Durham on a one-month trip, just a night in Durham on a 2- or 3-week trip.

For drivers with 48 hours between Edinburgh and York: leave Edinburgh early, tour Hadrian's Wall and the fort, take a walk and have lunch, and get to Durham in time to tour the cathedral and enjoy the 17:15 evensong service. Sleep in Durham. Tour Beamish or drive through the North York Moors the next day, arriving by late afternoon in York.

Durham

Without its cathedral, it would hardly be noticed. But with its cathedral, it's hard not to notice. Even from the train, it's a magnificent sight. Durham sits, seemingly happy to go nowhere along its river, under its castle and famous cathedral.

Orientation (tel. code: 0191)

Tidy little Durham clusters everything safely under its castle within the tight, protective bend of its river. The longest walk you'd make would be a 15-minute walk from the train station to the cathedral. It has a workaday, medieval, cobbled atmosphere and a scraggly peasant's market just off the main square.

Tourist Information

The TI, on the town square, often posts B&B vacancies on its door after hours (open Monday-Saturday 9:30-18:30, Sunday 14:00-17:00, tel. 0191/384-3720).

Durham

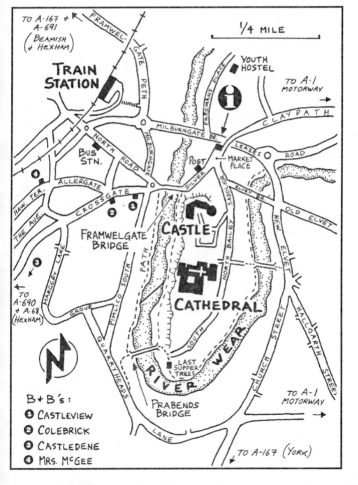

Sights—Durham

▲▲Durham Cathedral—Built to house the much-venerated bones of St. Cuthbert from Lindisfarne, the church is the best, least-altered Norman cathedral in England (free, 7:15-19:30 daily, less off-season, limited access during services). Study the difference between this heavy "Norman" (that's British for Romanesque) fortress of worship and the light-filled Gothics of later centuries. Let one of the many church attendants show you around. Pick up the 30p "walk about" guide, find the tombs of St. Cuthbert and Bede, and see the audiovisual introduction (50p, 11:00-15:00). The treasury is filled with medieval bits and holy pieces (£1, 10:00-16:30, Sunday 14:00-16:30). The view from the tower is worth the 325 steps (£1, 9:30-16:00, closed Sunday). There's also a good cafeteria.

For a thousand years this cradle of English Christianity has been praising God. To experience the cathedral in its intended context, go for an evensong service. Arrive early and ask to be seated in the choir. It's a spiritual Oz as 40 boys sing psalms—a red-and-white-robed pillow of praise, raised up by the powerful pipe organ. If you're lucky and the service went well, the organist runs a spiritual musical victory lap as the congregation breaks up. (No offering plates, no sermon, 17:15 almost nightly, 15:30 Sunday, normally not sung on Monday or when school term is out, tel. 091/386-2367.)

Riverside Walk—For a 20-minute woodsy escape, walk Durham's riverside path from Framwelgate Bridge to Prebends Bridge. Just between the Prebends Bridge and the old town, you'll find "The Upper Room," a cluster of trees carved to show the Last Supper when seen from the tree-trunk throne provided.

Sleeping in Durham
(£1 = about $1.50, tel code: 0191)

My recommended B&Bs are along Crossgate (from the city center, cross Framwelgate Bridge, take the first left, up the hill), a 5-minute walk from the town square and the train station. "Pay peanuts, get monkeys" places are along Claypath (over the highway from the TI). If you're driving into Durham on A690, you'll conveniently hit my recommended B&Bs.

Sleep code: **S**=Single, **D**=Double/Twin, **T**=Triple, **Q**=Quad, **B**=Bath/Shower, **WC**=Toilet, **CC**=Credit Card (**V**isa, **M**astercard, **A**mex).k

Colebrick B&B, meticulously run by Freda Mellanby, is a cozy, modern home with two double rooms for rent. Everything is super-comfortable and on the ground level (D-£42, solid beds, non-smoking, garden with cathedral views; 21 Crossgate, Durham DH1 4PS, tel. 384-9585). Husband Robin, son Stuart, and faithful dog Emma also help out.

Castleview Guest House, a block closer to the center, is bigger and creakier with seven comfortable rooms and a classy lounge (S-£20, D-£35, DB-£45, T-£40; 4 Crossgate, DH1 4PS, tel. 386-8852, Mike and Anne Williams).

Castledene B&B is tidy, simple, and friendly with three rooms and a TV lounge (S-£17, twin-£34; continue up Crossgate to Palatine View, cross the street, go up 10 steps to the pedestrian lane and walk 100 yards parallel to and above Crossgate Peth to the last house, 37 Nevilledale Terrace, tel. 384-8386, Lorna Byrne). **Mrs. McGee** rents decent rooms on a busier street closer to the station (S-£16, D-£32, T-£48; 53 Hawthorn Terrace, DH1 4EQ, tel. 384-7601).

The **Durham Castle** is a student residence actually on the castle grounds facing the cathedral. It rents 100 singles and 30 doubles to travelers from July through September (£18 per person, £21 with private facilities, meals served in an elegant dining hall; parking, with luck, on the cathedral green; tel. 374-3863). Request a room in the classy old main building. Otherwise you may get bomb-shelter-style modern dorm rooms.

Eating in Durham

For dinner, trust your host's advice. There are several interesting places in the town center. **Shaheens** in the old post office, up Saddler Street, serves good Indian meals with a healthy twist, nightly from 18:00. **The Stones**, on Silver Street, is a trendy 1960s burger place. **The Dragon**, out Claypath, serves good pub grub. **The Duke of Wellington,** serving great (and big-enough-for-two) meals in great pub atmosphere, is worth the drive (1½ miles down the A1050/ Darlington Road).

Train Connections
Durham to: Edinburgh (5/day, 2 hrs), **York** (11/day, 1 hr), **London** (9/day, 3 hrs), **Newcastle** (2/day, 20 min for buses to Hadrian's Wall).

Parking in Durham
While there are a few parking spots right on the cathedral green, parking in old Durham is miserable. For a short stop, use the high-rise parking garage in the town center. From the garage's seventh floor, a walkway takes you right into the old town. Parking at my recommended B&Bs, a short walk from the center of Durham, is easy.

Sights—Near Durham
▲▲**Beamish Open-Air Museum**—This huge, unique center energetically takes its visitors back to turn-of-the-century Northumbria. You'll need at least 3 hours to explore the 1900s town, train station, school, mining camp, and working farm. This isn't wax. If you touch the exhibits, they may smack you. Attendants at each stop explain everything, and an old tramway shuttles you through the huge park, saving wear and tear on your feet (£7; daily 10:00 -17:00, mid-July through August, last tickets 2 hours before closing, winter until 16:00, closed winter Mondays and Fridays; tel. 01207/231811). Unique in its coverage of the dawn of our century, Beamish is a former "European museum of the year."

Shuttle buses run hourly between downtown Durham and the Beamish Museum, 8 miles away. The museum is well signposted, located between the villages of Stanley and Chester-le-Street.

▲▲▲**Hadrian's Wall**—This is one of England's most thought-provoking sights. During the reign of Emperor Hadrian, the Romans built this great stone wall around A.D. 130 to protect England from invading Scottish tribes. Stretching 74 miles from coast to coast, it was defended by nearly 20,000 troops. Flanked by ditches, with castles every mile, the wall was built 15 feet high and wide enough to allow chariots to race from castle to castle. Today, several chunks of the wall, ruined forts, and museums thrill history buffs.

By far the best single stop is the Housesteads Fort with its fine museum, national park information center, and the

Durham and Northeast England

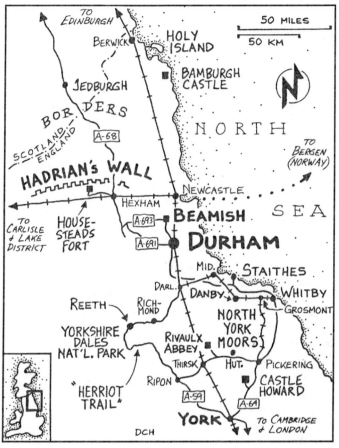

best-preserved segment of the wall, surrounded by powerful scenery (£2.20, fort open daily 10:00-18:00, shorter hours off-season, with car park and snack bar, tel. 01434/344525; when information center closes at 17:00, the car park becomes dangerous). From Housesteads, hike west along the wall speaking Latin. Vindolanda, a larger Roman fort and museum, is just south of the wall and worth a visit only if you've devoured the Housesteads museum and are still hungry (tel. 01434/344363).

For a good 3-mile walk, go from Steel Rigg (take the little road up from the Twice Brewed Pub) east along the crag and wall, past the mile castle sitting in a nick in the crag (castle #39, called Castle Nick), to Housesteads.

To sleep literally up against the wall, the **Sewing Shields Farm B&B** is a great value (S-£15, D-£30, and a quad, family deals, evening meals; run by friendly Lyn Murray, just east of Housesteads Fort, Haydon Bridge, Hexham, NE47 6NW, tel. 01434/684418). The nearby **Mile Castle Pub** cooks up all sorts of exotic game and offers the best dinner around, according to hungry National Park rangers. Two miles west of Housesteads, the **Twice Brewed Pub and Hotel** (S-£17, D-£34, plain dreary rooms, lots of singles, rarely full, tel. 01434/344534) serves decent pub grub nightly to a local crowd. The comfortable **Once Brewed Youth Hostel** (£8 per bed, with breakfast, 4 to 7 beds per room, tel. 01434/344360) is just next to the Twice Brewed Pub.

To reach Hadrian's Wall, catch a train from Durham to Newcastle (12/day, 20 min.), then head east on the Newcastle-Carlisle line (6/day). Get off at Bardon Mill (about a 45-min trip), the stop nearest Housesteads Fort. In summer, tour buses zip between Newcastle and Hadrian's Wall (4/day). By car, before Hexham (east of Newcastle) roller-coaster 2 miles down A6079 to B6318, following the Roman wall westward. Notice the wall and its trenches on either side. After 10 minutes on B6318 and several "severe dips" (if there's a certified nerd or bozo in the car, these road signs add a lot to a photo portrait), pull into the Housesteads Roman Fort information center. The Roman fort is on the right.

▲**Whitby**—Whitby (on the coast of the North York Moors) is a fun resort town with a busy harbor, steep and salty old streets, and a carousel of Coney Island-type amusements. It has lots of B&Bs, a great abbey (next door to a good **youth hostel** with 70 beds in 10 rooms, £7 per bed, closed 10:00-17:00, tel. 01947/602878), and a colorful people scene. **Pannett House** is a good value, renting nine rooms, a 10- or 15-minute walk from the harbor action (S-£13, D-£26, T-£39; 14 Normanby Terrace, tel. 01947/603261, Val and Allan Perks). TI tel. 01947/602674. Five buses daily from York (2 hrs, tel. 01653/692556).

▲**Staithes**—Captain James Cook's boyhood town, this is a salty tumble of cottages bunny-hopping down a ravine into a tiny harbor. Fishermen still outnumber tourists in undiscovered Staithes. The only reason I'd go to Staithes is to spend the night. The charming 200-year old **Coble Cottage** rents four twin rooms on the waterfront (D-£34, £30 for a 2-night stay, 3 Church Street, tel. 01947/840297, Maureen and Ken Hart). The **Harborside Guest House**, also on the waterfront, provides basic beds and the sound of waves to lull you to sleep (D-£38, 4 rooms, tel. 01947/841296). There's good bar food at the Royal George on High Street. The Endeavour Restaurant, also right downtown, is even better. Staithes, a short drive north of Whitby, is worthwhile by car. There are hourly 30-minute bus rides from Whitby to Staithes.

▲**Holy Island and Bamburgh**—This is the Holy Island of Lindisfarne Gospels fame. Twelve hundred years ago, this was Christianity's toehold on England. It's a pleasant visit, a quiet town with an evocative priory and striking castle (not worth touring), reached by a 2-mile causeway that's cut off daily by high tides. Tidal charts are posted, warning you when this holy place becomes Holy Island and you become stranded (for tide information, tel. 01289/307283). For a peaceful overnight, a few good B&Bs cluster in the town center (**Britannia Guest House**, D-£26, DB-£32, 4 rooms, tel. 01289/89218).

Holy Island is a short bus ride from Berwick, a town 70 minutes north of Durham on the London-Edinburgh train line. A few miles farther south down the coast from Holy Island is the grand **Bamburgh Castle,** overlooking the loveliest stretch of beach in Britain. Its impressive interior is worth touring (£2.50, daily 12:00-17:00, April-October, tel. 01668/214208). Berwick TI, tel. 01289/330733.

EDINBURGH

Edinburgh, the colorful city of Robert Louis Stevenson, Walter Scott, and Robert Burns, is Scotland's showpiece and one of Europe's most entertaining cities. Historical, monumental, fun and well-organized, it's a tourist's delight.

Take a royal hike down the Royal Mile through the old town. Historic, fascinating buildings pack the Royal Mile between the castle (on the top) and Holyrood Palace (on the bottom). Medieval skyscrapers stand shoulder-to-shoulder, hiding peaceful little courtyards connected to High Street by narrow lanes or even tunnels. This colorful jumble, in its day the most crowded city in the world, is the tourist's Edinburgh.

Edinburgh (ED'n-burah) was once two towns divided by a lake. To alleviate crowding, the lake was drained and a magnificent Georgian city, today's New Town, was laid out to the north. Georgian Edinburgh, like the city of Bath, shines with broad boulevards, straight streets, square squares, circular circuses, and elegant mansions decked out in colonnades, pediments, and sphinxes in the proud, neoclassical style of 200 years ago.

Planning Your Time
While the major sights can be seen in a day, on a 3-week tour of Britain, I'd give Edinburgh 2 days.

Day 1: Orient yourself with a Guide Friday bus tour. Do the whole loop, getting off only to tour the Georgian House. After touring the castle, grab a quick lunch on the Royal Mile. Catch the 14:00 walking tour of the Royal Mile. If you decide to tour Holyrood Palace do it after your walk, at about 16:00.

Day 2: Climb Sir Walter Scott Memorial for a city view; tour the National Gallery. Spend the rest of the day on the Royal Mile museum-going, shopping, or taking the "City, Sea, and Hills" bus tour. Evening: Scottish show, folk pub, or haunted walk.

Orientation (tel. code: 0131)

In the center of Edinburgh are a lovely park and Waverley Bridge where you'll find the TI, Waverley Shopping and Eating Center, train station, bus info office, the starting point for most city bus tours, festival office, the National Gallery, and a covered dance and music pavilion.

Tourist Information

The crowded tourist office (central as can be atop the Waverley Market on Princes Street, 9:00-20:00, Sunday 11:00-20:00, shorter hours and closed Sunday in off-season, tel. 0131/557-1700) has become a profit-seeking business with advice colored by who gives the best commissions. Ideally, skip it and telephone if you have questions. Their misnamed *Essential Guide to Edinburgh* (which costs 25p and shuffles a little information between lots of ads) has a cruddy little map. *The List*, the best monthly entertainment listing, is sold at newsstands. The TI's room-finding service bloats prices to get its cut. "Platform 19," another room-finding service in the station, is a little better—but there's no reason to use either. Call your B&B direct. For real information without the sales push, take advantage of the **Old Town Information Centre** at the Tron Church, where South Bridge hits the Royal Mile. They have a great free map of the Royal Mile. A couple of blocks down the Mile at 5 Blackfriars Street, the Backpackers' Centre is also a good source of information.

Trains and Buses

Arriving by train puts you in the city center a few steps from the TI and bus to my recommended B&Bs. Train info tel. 556-2451. Both National Express (tel. 452-8777) and Scottish Citylink (tel. 557-5717) buses use the bus station a block from the train station in the Georgian town on St. Andrew Square.
The Edinburgh Airport is close to town and well connected by shuttle buses (4/hr, £3.20, flight info: tel. 344-3302)

Getting Around

City buses are handy and inexpensive (LRT information office at the corner of Waverley Bridge and Market Street,

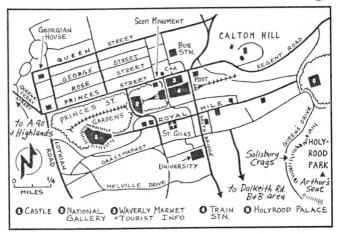

Edinburgh

● CASTLE ● NATIONAL GALLERY ● WAVERLY MARKET + TOURIST INFO ● TRAIN STN. ● HOLYROOD PALACE

info tel. 220-4111, average fare 55p, tell the driver where you're going, drop exact change into box or lose the excess, grab your ticket as you board, and push the stop button so your stop isn't skipped). Taxis are reasonable (easy to flag down, several handy pick-up points, 90p drop charge, 60p extra after 18:00, average ride between downtown and B&B district—£2.50). Nearly all Edinburgh sights are within walking distance.

Banking
Barclays has decent rates and no 2 percent charge if you have Barclays or "interpayment" bank checks (9:30-17:00, 50 meters into new town from TI and station at 18 South Andrew St).

Sights—Along the Royal Mile
(In walking order from top to bottom.)

▲▲▲**Royal Mile**—This is one of Europe's most interesting historic walks. Follow a local guide (daily at 10:00, 11:00 and 14:00, often free during the festival, £4 other times, see below) or do it yourself with a Royal Mile guidebook. Each step of the way is entertaining. Start at the top and loiter down to the palace. I've listed the top sights of the Royal Mile—working downhill.

The Royal Mile is actually a series of different streets in a straight line. All along, you'll find interesting shops, cafés, and closes (lanes leading to tiny squares), providing the thoughtful visitor a few little rough edges of the old town. See it now. In a few years, it will be a string of tourist gimmicks, woolen shops, and contrived "sights."

▲▲**Edinburgh Castle**—The fortified birthplace of the city 1,300 years ago, this is the imposing symbol of Edinburgh. Start with the free 30-minute guided introduction tour (every 20 minutes from entry, see clock for the next departure). See the Scottish National War Memorial, the Banqueting Hall with fine Scottish Crown Jewels, the room full of Battle of Culloden mementos, St. Margaret's Chapel (oldest building in town), the giant cannon, and the city view from the ramparts (in that order). Allow 90 minutes, including the tour. (£5, 9:30-18:00, until 17:00 in winter and on holidays, tel. 244-3101, cafeteria.)

The Scotch Whiskey Heritage Centre is only for the desperate. Even with little whiskey kegs for train cars and toilets that actually got the "Loo of the Year" award, the Whiskey ride is a rip-off designed to distill £4 out of your pocket. The Camera Obscura across the street is just as rewarding.

▲▲**Gladstone's Land**—Take a good look at this typical 16th- to17th-century house, complete with lived-in furnished interior and guides in each room who love to talk. (£2.50, April-October 10:00-17:00, Sunday 14:00-17:00, good Royal Mile photo from the top-floor window or from the top of its entry stairway through the golden eagle.)

▲**Lady Stair's House/Writers' Museum**—This interesting house, which dates back to 1622, is filled with manuscripts and knickknacks of Scotland's three greatest literary figures:

Royal Mile

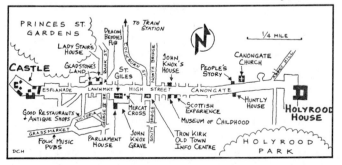

Robert Burns, Sir Walter Scott, and Robert Louis Stevenson. Worth a few minutes for anyone, fascinating for fans (free, 10:00-18:00, till 17:00 off-season, closed Sunday).

Deacon Brodies' Tavern—A decent place for a light meal (see below); read the story of its notorious namesake on the wall facing Bank Street.

▲**St. Giles Cathedral**—Don't miss this engaging Gothic church's ornate, medieval thistle chapel (to the right of the altar, 50p) or the Scottish crown steeple on top (daily 9:00-19:00, until 17:00 off-season, fine café downstairs). John Knox, founder of austere Scottish Presbyterianism, is buried out back, austerely, under the parking lot (spot 44).

The Parliament House—Stop in to see the grand hall with its fine hammer-beamed ceiling and stained glass (free, public welcome). For a trip into the 18th century, drop by Tuesday through Friday around 10:00 or 10:30, the best time to see all the wigged and robed legal beagles hard at work. Greater eminence . . . longer wig. You are welcome to observe trials in action (10:00-16:00). The doorman is helpful (entry behind St. Giles Church near parking spot 21, open daily).

Museum of Childhood is a 5-story playground of historical toys and games (free, 10:00-18:00, till 17:00 off-season, closed Sundays).

John Knox's House—Fascinating for Reformation buffs. This fine 16th-century house is filled with things from the life of the Great Reformer. (£1.25, 10:00-16:30, firmly closed on Sunday.)

▲**Scottish Experience and Living Craft Centre**—This commercial venture actually fills a void and, for many, makes an entertaining visit. You'll see several crafts in action (bagpipe-making, weaving, kilt-making) and a computerized study-your-clan center. The tiny theater (£1) continuously runs two videos on Edinburgh or Scotland and is ringed by an exhibit on Highland dress (free, 10:00-18:00, tel. 557-9350, home of recommended Scottish Evening, described below).

People's Story is an interesting exhibition tracing the lot of the working class through the 18th, 19th, and 20th centuries (free, 10:00-18:00, till 17:00 off-season, closed Sundays).

▲**Huntly House**—Another old house full of old stuff, worth a look for its early Edinburgh history and handy ground-floor WC. Don't miss the copy of the National Covenant written on an animal skin or the sketches of pre-Georgian Edinburgh with its lake still wet (free, 10:00-18:00, closed Sunday).

▲**Holyrood Palace**, at the bottom end of the Royal Mile, is where the Queen stays when she's in town. On a mandatory guided tour, see the royal apartments, state apartment, lots of rich furnishings, paintings, and history (£3.50, 9:30-18:00, Sunday 10:30-16:30, closed when the Queen's home, tel. 556-7371).

Bonnie Wee Other Sights

▲**Walter Scott Monument**—Built in 1840, this elaborate, neo-Gothic monument honors the great author, one of Edinburgh's many illustrious sons. Climb 287 steps for a royal view of the Royal Mile (£1, 9:00-18:00, until 17:00 off-season, closed Sunday).

▲▲**Georgian House** is a trip back to 1796. This refurbished Georgian house comes with a volunteer guide in each room trained in the force-feeding of stories and trivia. Start your visit with the interesting video (£3, 10:00-17:00, Sunday 14:00-17:00, at 7 Charlotte Square). From this museum, walk through Georgian Edinburgh. The grand George Street, connecting St. Andrew and Charlotte Squares, was the centerpiece of the elegantly planned New Town.

Princes Street Gardens—This grassy former lake-bed separates Edinburgh's new and old towns with a wonderful escape from the city-ness of it all. There are plenty of concerts and dances in the summer and the oldest floral clock in the world. Join local office workers for a picnic-lunch break.

National Gallery—An elegant Neoclassical building with a small, but impressive, collection of European masterpieces and the best look you'll get at Scottish paintings (free, 10:00-17:00, Sunday 14:00-17:00, tel. 556-8921).

▲▲**Walking Tours**—Several competitive and hard-working little companies do Royal Mile (usually 10:00, 11:00 and 14:00) and Ghost walks (usually 19:00 and 21:00). Tours are about 1½ to 2 hours long and cost £4. Pick up brochures for Robin's (start at TI, tel. 661-0125) and Mercat (meet 30 minutes early at the TI for those who can't find Mercat Cross on the Royal Mile, tel. 661-4541). The Royal Mile tour is most important. These entertaining tours are led by guides who enjoy making a short story long. They ignore the big sights, taking you behind the scenes with piles of barely historic gossip, bully-pulpit Scottish pride, and fun but forgettable trivia. The evening walks, more than a pile of ghost stories, are an entertaining and cheap night out. You can also rent **audio tape tours** (£4, from Tolbooth Church near castle, drop walkman near palace) for an hour-long professional narration-with-music that walks you the length of the Mile and offers little more than the information you already have in your hands. (Audio tours can also be rented at the Tron Church Old Town Information Centre.)

▲**Hop-on and Hop-off City Bus Tours**—Guide Friday (£5.50, tel. 556-2244) and LRT's "Edinburgh Classic Tour" (£4.50, tel. 220-4111) both circle the town center—Waverley Bridge, around the castle, Royal Mile, Calton Hill, Georgian town, and Princes Street—in about an hour with pick-ups about every 15 minutes and an informative narration. You can stop and go all day on one ticket. Overlapping can be interesting, since each guide has her own story to tell. On sunny days they go topless (the buses), but can suffer from traffic noise and congestion.

City Bus Tours—Several all-day bus tours can take you as far as Loch Ness. Tours leave from near the train station. "City, Sea, and Hills" is the best 90-minute tour of greater Edinburgh (£3, information at LRT office, on Waverley Bridge, tel. 220-4111).

Royal Commonwealth Games Swimming Pool—The biggest pool I've ever seen. Open to the public, good Café Aqua overlooking the pool, weights, saunas, and plenty of water rides, including Europe's biggest "flume" or water slide (£1.75, Monday-Friday 9:00-21:00, Saturday and Sunday 8:00-19:00, tel. 667-7211). If you'd rather be skiing, there's an open-all-year hill covered with brush, with a chairlift, T-bar, and rentable skis, boots, and poles, on the edge of town (daily 9:30-21:00, tel. 445-4433).

▲**Arthur's Seat**—A 30-minute hike up the 822-foot volcanic mountain (surrounded by a fine park overlooking Edinburgh), starting from the Holyrood Palace or the Commonwealth Pool, gives you a rewarding view. It's the easiest "I climbed a mountain" feeling I've ever had. You can drive up most of the way from behind; follow the one-way street from the palace (park by the little lake).

Greyhound Races—This is a pretty lowbrow scene. But if you've never seen dog racing, this is a memorable night out combining great dog- and people-watching with a chance to lose some money gambling. Races are held about two nights a week at Powderhall Stadium.

Edinburgh Crystal—Blowing, molding, cutting, polishing, engraving, the Edinburgh Crystal Company glassworks tour smashes anything you'll see in Venice. The 35-minute tours start at regular intervals between 9:15 and 15:30, Monday-Friday (£2, children under age 8 and large dogs are not allowed in for safety reasons). There is a shop full of "bargain" second-quality pieces, a video show, and a good cafeteria. (Free red minibus shuttle service from Waverley Bridge departs 10:00, 11:00, 12:00, 14:00, and 15:00 in summer, or drive 10 miles south of town on A701 to Penicuik. Call first, tel. 01968/675128.)

Stirling Castle—It's popular but currently used as a barracks, and nowhere near as interesting as Edinburgh's castle. The town is pleasantly medieval, however, and many commute (1 hour by train) to the more hectic Edinburgh from here. (TI tel. 01786/475019.)

▲▲▲**The Edinburgh Festival**—One of Europe's great cultural events, Edinburgh's annual festival turns the city into a carnival of culture. There are enough music, dance, art, drama, and multicultural events to make even the most jaded tourist get frisky and drool with excitement. Every day is jammed with formal and spontaneous fun. The official and fringe festivals rage from mid-August through early September (August 13-September 2 in 1995, August 11-31 in 1996), with the Military Tattoo starting a week earlier. Many city sights run on extended hours, and those that normally close on Sundays, don't. It's a glorious time to be in Edinburgh.

The official festival is more formal and serious, with entertainment by festival invitation only. Although major events sell out well in advance, 50 seats are held to be sold at 8:00 on the day of the show at the show office at 21 Market Street (£4-£35, major credit cards accepted, booking from April on, tel. 225-5756).

The less formal, "on the edge" comedy and theater, Fringe Festival (ticket and info office just below St. Giles Cathedral on the Royal Mile, tel. 226-5259, bookings tel. 226-5138) has hundreds of events and, it seems, more performers than viewers. Tickets are usually available at the door.

The Military Tattoo is a massing of the bands, drums, and bagpipes with groups from all over what was the British Empire. Displaying military finesse with a stirring lone-piper finale, this grand spectacle fills the castle esplanade nightly except Sunday, normally from a week before the festival starts until a week before it finishes (£8-£15, major credit cards accepted, booking starts in January, tel. 225-1188, Friday and Saturday shows sell out, Monday-Thursday shows rarely do). If nothing else, it is a really big show.

If you do manage to hit Edinburgh during the festival, extend your stay by a day or two and book a room far in advance. While fringe tickets and most Tattoo tickets are available the day of the show, you may want to book an official event or two in advance. Do it direct and easy by telephone, leaving your credit-card number. You can pick up your ticket at the office the day of the show. Several publications list and evaluate festival events, including the festival's official schedule, the *Festival Times*, *The List*, *Fringe Program*, and the *Daily Diary*.

Shopping—The best shopping is along Princes Street (don't miss elegant old Jenner's Department Store), Victoria Street (antiques galore), and the Royal Mile (touristy but competitively priced, shops usually open 9:00-17:30, later on Thursday).

Entertainment in Edinburgh

▲**Scottish folk evenings**—These £25 to £30 dinner shows, are generally for tour groups, held in huge halls of expensive hotels. (Prices are bloated to include 20% commissions, without which, the show don't go on.) You get a "traditional" meal followed by a full slate of swirling kilts, blaring bagpipes, and colorful Scottish folk dancing with an "old-time music hall"-type master of ceremonies. **Prince Charlie's Extravaganza** at The Scottish Experience (described above), across from John Knox's house on the Royal Mile, is a fun show. It's too small for a massing of the tour groups (about 60 seats), smoke-free (thank goodness, you're pretty packed in), and serves a decent four-course meal (Scotch broth, haggis with neeps and tatties, and a beef pastry with vegetables, wine, ice cream and coffee, vegetarian alternatives available). The dancing and music (piping, accordion, singing) are good, and if you reserve directly showing this book you get a 20 percent discount off the £25 price (meal at 19:00, show starts at 19:30, and you sing "Auld Lang Syne" by 22:00, shows nearly nightly, tel. 557-9350). The boss, Mike Boyle, promised this special price for 1995.

▲**Folk music in pubs**—For an informal evening of folk music, head on down to Grassmarket (below the castle) and find the right pub. The Fiddlers Arms (tel. 229-2665), White Hart Inn, and Black Bull, among others, regularly feature live folk music. Preservation Hall (a block away on Victoria Street, tel. 226-3816) has live jazz and rock on many Thursday, Friday, and Saturday nights. Just off the Royal Mile on Cockburn Street, the Malt Shovel Pub is a typical Edinburgh pub with impromptu folk and jazz most nights and the best selection of malt whiskey in town (225-6843). My favorite Scottish band, the North Sea Gas, plays every Friday and many Saturdays (20:30-23:00, free) at Platform One in the Caledonian Hotel on Princes Street. The Edinburgh Folk Club, which meets at the Bistro Bar Wednesday evenings (£4, near Princes Street, tel. 557-4792), is a good bet for traditional music and dancing.

Sleeping in Edinburgh
(£1 = about $1.50, tel. code: 0131)
The annual festival fills the city every year in the last half of August (August 13-September 2 in 1995). Conventions, school holidays, and other surprises can make room-finding tough at almost any time. If you don't call in advance you'll probably end up paying 30 percent extra for a relative dump. The good places are a fine value; the rest are depressing. Downtown hotels are overpriced (minimum £70 doubles). For the best prices, book direct and call in advance! Going direct (rather than through the greedy TI), you're likely to get the best price. When a room has no "en suite facilities," they are usually a tissue toss away.

My favorite B&B district, where you'll find all these recommendations, is south of town near the Royal Commonwealth Pool, just off Dalkeith Road. This com-

Edinburgh, Our Neighborhood

fortably safe neighborhood is a 20-minute walk or short bus
ride from the Royal Mile. All listings are on quiet streets, a
2-minute walk from a bus stop, and well-served by city buses.
Near the B&Bs, you'll find plenty of eateries, easy free parking, and a handy laundromat (Monday-Friday 8:30-17:00,
Saturday and Sunday 10:00-14:30, £2.50 for a self-serve load;
ask about drop-off-and-pick-up service, 208 Dalkeith Road,
tel. 667-0825).

From the station, TI, or Scott Monument cross Princes
Street and wait under the C&A sign (buses #21, #33, #82,
#C11, or #86, 60p, exact change or pay more, ride 10 min-
utes to first stop 100 yards after the Pool, push the button).
These buses also stop at North Bridge and High Street on
the Royal Mile. Prices may vary with the seasonal demand.

Sleep code: **S**=Single, **D**=Double/Twin, **T**=Triple,
Q=Quad, **B**=Bath/Shower, **WC**=Toilet, **CC**=Credit Card
(**V**isa, **M**astercard, **A**mex).

Millfield Guest House, run by Liz and Ed Broomfield, is thoughtfully furnished with antique class, a rare sit-and-chat ambience, and a comfy TV lounge. Since the showers are down the hall, you'll get spacious rooms and great prices (S-£15.50 to £16.50, D-£31 to £33, T-£46 to £49 for direct bookings only; good beds, absolutely no smoking, quiet but friendly, CC:VM, easy reservation with CC which lets you arrive late; 12 Marchhall Road, EH16 5HR, tel. 031/667-4428). Decipher the breakfast prayer by Robert Burns. See how many stone (14 lb) you weigh in the elegant throne room. This is worth calling well in advance.

The Belford House is tidy, simple, fresh, bright, friendly, and a fine value (D-£34, T-£51, family deals; 13 Blacket Avenue, tel. 667-2422, Mrs. Borthwick).

Ravensneuk Guest House is also good (D-£34 to £40 depending on room and season, DBWC-£50, family deals, great lounge, solid beds, some non-smoking rooms; 11 Blacket Ave., EH9 1RR, tel. 667-5347). Jeanette and Jim Learmonth rent five rooms in this quiet, comfortable, and very Victorian home.

Dunedin Guest House is bright and pastel, nearly non-smoking, and a good value for those who need a private bathroom (S-£20, DB-£38 to £42 depending on the season, family deals, 7 rooms, solid beds, TVs in rooms, Scotland and Edinburgh videos in lounge; 8 Priestfield Road, EH16 5HH, tel. 668-1949, Annette Preston).

Dorstan Private Hotel is small and personable, but professional and hotelesque with all the comforts. Several of its 14 prim rooms are on the ground floor. (DB-£56, DBWC-£62, family rooms, CC:VM; 7 Priestfield Road, EH16 5HJ, tel. 667-6721, fax 668-4644, Mairae Campbell).

Kenvie Guest House (one small twin-£30, D-£32, DB-£40; prices for direct bookings promised through 1995; family rooms; 16 Kilmaurs Rd., EH16 5DA, tel. 668-1964, easy telephone reservations, Dorothy Vidler) offers no-smoking rooms and lots of personal touches.

Priestville B&B (D-£30, DBWC-£36, priced for direct bookings through 1995, 10 Priestfield Road, tel. 667-2435, Audrey and Jim Christie) is a big old place, a little smoky, with charming rough edges and a friendly welcome.

These places are sleepable in the same fine neighborhood: **Highland Park House** (D-£32, 16 Kilmaurs Terrace, tel. 667-9204, Mrs. Cathy Kelly), and **Turret Guest House** (D-£34, DBWC-£42, 8 Kilmaurs Terrace, Mrs. Jackie Cameron, tel. 667-6704).

Sleeping in Dorms and Hostels

Although Edinburgh's youth hostels are well-run, open to all, and provide £8 bunk beds, an £8 savings over B&Bs, they include no breakfast and are comparatively scruffy. They are **The Bruntsfield Hostel** (on a park, 7 Bruntsfield Crescent, buses #11, #15, #16 to and from Princes St., tel. 447-2994); the **Edinburgh Hostel** (4 to 22 beds per room, 18 Eglinton Crescent, tel. 337-1120). The **High Street Independent Hostel** (8- to 10-bed rooms, young, hip, well-run, scruffy, videos, my mom wouldn't sleep a wink here, but my little sister would dig it, 50 yards off the Royal Mile; 8 Blackfriars St., tel. 557-3984, free historic walks many mornings, no membership needed) is perfectly located; bursting with user-friendly services; runs another place up the street; is a grapevine for shoestring, nose-ring travelers; and little old ladies have reportedly enjoyed a stay here. They are certainly welcome.

Eating in Edinburgh

Eating Along the Royal Mile

Historic pubs and doily cafés with reasonable, unremarkable meals abound. **Deacon Brodie's Pub** serves soup, sandwiches, and snacks on the ground floor and good £5 meals upstairs (daily 12:00-22:00, crowded after 20:00). For a cheap lunch in legal surroundings, try the cafeteria in the **Parliament House** (9:30-15:00, Monday-Friday, entry behind St. Giles church near parking spot 21). Or munch prayerfully in the **Lower Aisle** restaurant under St. Giles church (Monday-Friday 10:00-16:30). **Clarinda's Tea Room**, near the bottom of the Royal Mile, is also good (9:00-16:45 daily). **Dubh Prais Restaurant** serves decent Scottish food in a small, candlelit, stone-walled basement (£15 and up, reserve in advance, lunchtime and 18:30-22:30, closed Sunday and Monday; just below St. Giles Cathedral at 123b High Street, tel. 557-5732; chef/owner James

McWillians). On Victoria Street, consider the very French **Pierre Victoire** (£10 meals, lunch and 18:00-23:00, closed Sunday, #9 Victoria St, tel. 225-1721) or the upstairs café in the Byzantium antique mall, across the street from Pierre Victoire.

Eating in the New Town

The **Waverley Center Food Court**, below the TI and above the station, is a ring of flashy, trendy, fast-food joints (including Scot's Pantry for quick traditional edibles) littered with paper plates and shoppers. Edinburgh seems to be a lunching kind of place. Local office workers pile into **Lanterna** for good Italian food (family-run, fresh and friendly, 83 Hanover St., 2 blocks off Princes St., tel. 226-3090). Rose Street has tons of pubs.

Eating in Dalkeith Road Area, near Your B&B

Within a block of the corner of Newtington and Preston Streets are all kinds of little eateries. For a fun local atmosphere that makes up for the food, the **Wine Glass Pub**, serves filling "basket meals" (Sunday-Thursday, 18:00-20:30, £3.50. **Chinatown**, next to the Wine Glass, is moderate and good. The **Chatterbox** (8:30-20:00, down Preston St. from the big pool) is fine for a light meal with tea. For bad fish-and-chips, **Brattisanis** at 87 Newington Road is good. Skip the milkshakes, but if you need some cheap haggis, they've got it. The huge **Commonwealth Pool** has a noisy cafeteria for hungry swimmers and budget travelers (pass the entry without paying, sit with a poolside view).

Train Connections

Edinburgh to Inverness (7/day, 4 hrs), **York** (hrly, 2½ hrs), **London** (hrly, 5 hrs), **Durham** (hrly, 2 hrs), **Lake District** (train south past Carlisle to Penrith, catch a bus to Keswick; 6/day, 40-min trip).

Route Tips for Drivers

Driving into Edinburgh from the north: signs to "city centre" lead to the black, towering neo-Gothic Scott Memorial (near the castle). From there, drive down Princes Street, turn right over the North Bridge and follow the A68/Jedburgh signs to my recommended B&Bs, all just beyond the big, flat, white Royal Commonwealth Pool building on Dalkeith Road. (For most, take the first left off Dalkeith Road after the pool).

Edinburgh to Hadrian's Wall (100 miles) and Durham (150 miles): From Edinburgh, Dalkeith Road leads south, becoming A68 (handy supermarket on left as you leave Dalkeith Town, 10 minutes south of Edinburgh, parking behind store). A68 takes you to Hadrian's Wall in 2 hours. You'll pass Jedburgh and its abbey after 1 hour. (For one last shot of shop-Scotland, there's a coach tour's delight just before Jedburgh, with kilt-makers, woolens, and a sheepskin shop.) Across from Jedburgh's lovely abbey is a free parking lot, a good visitor's center, and public toilets. The England/ Scotland border (great view, Mr. Softy ice-cream and tea caravan) is a fun, quick stop. Before Hexham, roller-coaster 2 miles down A6079 to B6318, following the Roman wall westward. (See Hadrian's Wall for more driving instructions.)

OBAN AND THE HIGHLANDS

Filled with more natural and historical mystique than people, the Highlands are where you find extreme Scotland: legends of Bonnie Prince Charlie swirl around rotten castles as pipers and kilts swirl around tourists. The harbor of Oban is a fruit crate of Scottish traditions, and the Hebrides are just an island hop, skip, and jump away.

The Highlands are snipped in two by the impressive Caledonian canal, with Oban at one end and Inverness at the other. The major sights cluster along the scenic 120-mile stretch between the two towns. Oban is a fine home base for western Scotland and Inverness makes a good overnight stop on your way through eastern Scotland.

Planning Your Time

While Ireland has more charm and Wales has better sights, this area provides your best look at rural Scottish culture. It's a lot of miles but they're scenic and the roads are good. In two days you can get a feel for the area with the drive described below. To do the islands, you'll need more time. Iona is worthwhile, but adds a day to your trip. Generally, the region is hungry for the tourist dollar and everything overtly Scottish is that way to woo the tourist. You'll need more than a quick visit to get away from that. With a car and two days to connect the Lakes District and Edinburgh consider this plan:

Day 1: 9:00, short stop at the Castlerigg stone circle before leaving the Lake District; 13:00, lunch on Loch Lomond; joy-ride on, stopping briefly at Inveraray; 16:00, arrive in Oban, tour whiskey distillery, drop by the TI; 20:30, have dinner with music at McTavish's Kitchen.

Day 2: 9:00, leave Oban; 10:00, explore the valley of Glencoe; 11:00, drive to Fort Augustus; 12:00, follow Caledonian Canal, stopping at Loch Ness to take care of any monster business; 15:00, visit the evocative Culloden Battlefield near Inverness; 16:00, drive south; 19:00, set up in Edinburgh.

With more time, spend a second night in Oban and tour Iona or sleep in Inverness or Pitlochry, both fun towns.

Oban

Oban, called the "gateway to the isles," is a busy little ferry-and-train terminal with a charming shiver-and-bustle vitality that gives you a feel for small-town Scotland. Wind, boats, gulls, several layers of islands, and the promise of a wide-open Atlantic beyond give it a rugged and salty charm.

Orientation (tel. code: 01631)

There's nothing earth-shaking to see. The business action, just a couple of streets deep, stretches along the harbor and its promenade. The sights are close together and the town seems eager to please its many visitors. There's live, touristy music nightly in several bars and restaurants, shops sell woolen and tweed with cash registers cocked (open until 20:00 and on Sunday), and posters announce a variety of enticing day-tours to Scotland's wild and windblown western islands. The unfinished "colosseum" on the hill overlooking the town (McCaig's Tower, 1897) was an "employ the workers and build me a fine memorial" project undertaken by an early Oban tycoon.

Tourist Information

The TI has brochures listing everything from saunas to launderettes to horse-riding to rainy-day activities, and a fine bookshop (just off the harbor in the center a block from the train station, Monday-Saturday, 9:00-20:45, Sunday 9:00-17:00, shorter hours outside of July and August, tel. 63122). The train and bus stations are between the TI and the waterfront.

Sights—Oban

▲West Highland Malt Scotch Whiskey Distillery Tours—The Oban whiskey distillery, which celebrated its 200th birthday in 1994, produces 14,000 liters a week. They offer serious and fragrant 40-minute, £2 tours explaining the process from start to finish, with a free, smooth sample in the middle and a discount coupon for the shop at the end. The free exhibition preceding the tour gives a quick history of Scotland and its whiskey. This is the handiest whiskey tour you'll see, just a block off the harbor (Monday-Friday and in-season Saturday, 9:30-17:00, last tour at 16:15; to

Oban

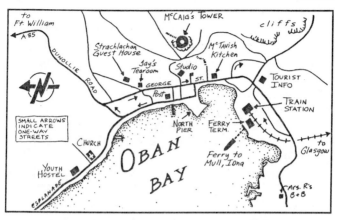

avoid a very long wait, call to reserve a place, tel. 64262).
Tour Iona and Mull—For the best one-day look at the
dramatic and historic Hebrides island scenery around Oban,
take one of several Iona/Mull tours offered in Oban. The
Isle of Mull, the third largest in Scotland, has 300 scenic
miles of coastline, a castle, and a 3,169-foot-high mountain.
The stark, historic, and car-free island of Iona is connected
to the western tip of Mull by a tiny regular ferry. St.
Columba brought Christianity to Scotland via the Iona Abbey
in A.D. 590. Near the abbey is a 13th-century Benedictine
nunnery, a burial place of ancient kings, an ecumenical
community, a museum, and a few shops, pubs, and B&Bs.

The island tours include the Oban-Mull ferry (40 min),
an entertaining and informative bus ride across the Isle of
Mull (90 min), the small ferry connection to Iona (10 min),
time to roam on Iona (2 hrs), and a return to Oban via ferry
(£14 on Bowman's, 10:00-17:30, best in fair weather, tel.
63221). Some companies offer flexible schedules if you want
more time in Mull or an extension to the wildly scenic Isle of
Staffa with Fingal's Cave. Guides are local boys who know
how to spin a yarn, making historical trivia fascinating, or at
least fun. There are several tours and companies to choose
from. Taking your car onto the ferry is very expensive (at
least £20 each way).
Kerrera—This stark but very green island, opposite Oban,
offers a quick, easy opportunity to get that romantic island

experience (£2 round-trip, upon request, at Gallanach's dock, 2 miles south of Oban).

Isle of Seil—Enjoy a walk, solitude, and the sea. Drive 15 miles south of Oban to the Isle of Seil, connected to the mainland by a bridge (for more info, see Eating, below).

Sleeping in Oban
(£1 = about $1.50, tel. code: 01631)

Sleep code: **S**=Single, **D**=Double/Twin, **T**=Triple, **Q**=Quad, **B**=Bath/Shower, **WC**=Toilet, **CC**=Credit Card (Visa, Mastercard, Amex).

Strathlachlan Guest House—This is a winner. Mrs. Rena Anderson's place is stocking-feet cozy, crackerjack friendly, and chocolate-box tidy. It's a spacious, uncluttered place with six rooms, solid beds, a great TV lounge, easy parking, and a good central location 2 blocks off the water just past Jay's Tearoom, 5 minutes' walk from the train station (S-£14, D-£28, T-£42, Q-£56, family deals; 2 Strathaven Terrace, Oban, Argyll, tel. 63861).

Tanglin B&B, next door, is another fine value. Liz and Jim Montgomery offer a bright and brand-new-feeling place with springy beds, TVs in the rooms, and an easygoing atmosphere (S-£13, D-£26, DB-£32, ask about off-season rates and family deals on larger rooms; 3 Strathaven Terrace, tel. 63247). The **Raniven Guest House** (D-£32, DB-£37.50, some non-smoking rooms, 2 nights minimum, Strathlachlan Terrace, tel. 62713), **MacColl's B&B** (S-£15, D-£30, firm beds, noisy street; around the corner on Dunollie Road, tel. 65361), and **Glenara B&B** (no smoking, run by Dorothy Bingham, 3 blocks off the waterfront on Rockfield Rd, tel. 63172) are sleepable.

The **Barriemore Hotel** is the last place (and only good value) on Oban's grand waterfront "Esplanade." It's a bit smoky, but has a classy, dark, woody, equestrian feel with 15 spacious and comfortable rooms furnished like living rooms (DB-£40 to £52, CC:VM, firm beds, grand views, some easy access ground-floor rooms; The Esplanade, PA34 5AQ, tel. 66356, Evelyn and Jim McLean).

The **youth hostel**, on the Esplanade alongside the finest hotels in town, is in a grand building with a smashing harbor/island view (£8 per bed with sheets, non-members of any age welcome for £1.50 extra, 4- to 16-bed rooms, great facilities and public rooms, closed winter, tel. 62025). Just a block from the TI and train station, and normally filled with backpackers in summer, is the **Jeremy Inglis B&B** (£7 per bed in basic, shared rooms with a continental breakfast; 21 Airds Crescent, Oban, tel. 65065 or 63064).

Just south of town, **Mrs. Robertson's B&B** is a mini-estate in a lush garden with a commanding view of the bay and islands. She rents a twin and a double (DB-£35; Dungrianach, Pulpit Hill, Oban, Argyll, PA34 4LX, tel. 62840). From the TI, go up Albany Street and take the second right up Pulpit Hill. When the road levels in a forest, turn right at the Dungrianach sign a half-block before a telephone booth.

Eating (with Swirling Kilts) in Oban

To mix a folk show inexpensively with dinner, eat at **McTavish's Kitchen**. Facing the harbor on central George Street, this huge eating hall (non-smokers get the best harbor views) is an Oban institution featuring live, but tired, folk music and dancing nightly (mid-May through September). This is your basic tourist trap (as is virtually anything so traditionally Scottish), filled mostly with English vacationers. The food is inexpensive and edible (£5 for a basic plate, £13 for the super Scottish multi-course menu). The piping, dancing, and singing happen nightly from 20:30-22:30 (the three-person band plays the hour-long cycle twice, so you'll cover all the cultural bases in an hour). The show costs £3 without a meal, £1.50 with dinner, or free with dinner with a coupon from your B&B. No reservations required.

Jay's Tearoom, near my recommended B&Bs on George Street, is an elegant pastel teahouse humid with happy eaters. Open nightly until 22:00, it's a good place to try the Scottish equivalent of rice and beans: "haggis, tatties and neeps." (Haggis, my waitress admitted, is on the menu just for tourists. Like most young Scots, she had never tried it.)

The Studio is a small, candlelit restaurant featuring serious first-class Scottish cooking (£11 for a full Scottish meal, 17:00-22:00 nightly, tel. 62030). It has a real hit-the-spot-on-a-stormy-day prawn-and-clam chowder and great trout.

For an interesting drive and dinner, head south from Oban on A816 to B844. Just over the bridge, on the Isle of Seil, is a pub called **Tigh-an-Truish** ("house of trousers"). After a 1745 English law forbade kilts on the mainland, Highlanders used this pub to change from kilts to trousers before crossing the bridge. The Tigh-an-Truish pub serves great meals to those in kilts or pants (meals daily 12:00-14:15, 18:00-20:30, darts anytime, good seafood dish, crispy vegetables, tel. 01852/300242). Five miles across the island on a teeny second island 300 yards beyond is Easdale, a historic, touristy, windy, little slate-mining town facing the open Atlantic (tiny shuttle ferry, tiny slate-town museum, incredibly tacky egomaniac's "Highland Arts" shop).

Transportation Connections
Oban to: Inverness (6 buses/day, 4 hrs), **Glasgow** (4 trains/day, 3 hrs). **Glasgow-Edinburgh** trains (2/hr, 1 hr), **Glasgow-Penrith** (9/day, 2 hrs, 6 buses/day from there to Keswick, Lakes District). Ferries fan out from Oban to the **southern Hebrides**. Train info (tel. 63083), bus info (tel. 62856) and Caledonian MacBrayne Ferry info (tel. 62285).

The Highlands: From Oban to Inverness
Discover Glencoe's dark secrets in the Weeping Glen as Britain's highest peak, Ben Nevis, keeps its head in the clouds. Explore the locks and lochs of the Caledonian canal while the Loch Ness monster plays hide-and-seek. Hear the music of the Highlands in Inverness and the echo of muskets in Culloden, where the English defeated Bonnie Prince Charlie and his Scottish hopes.

Getting Around
Forget about trains and hop on buses. Six buses a day connect the towns from Oban to Inverness (4 hrs). Ask at the station for the exact schedule and stops so you can visit sights along the way, catching a later bus as you go.

Sights—Highlands
▲▲**Glencoe** is the essence of the wild, powerful, and stark beauty of the Highlands (and, I think, excuses the hurried tourist from needing to go north of Inverness). Along with

Oban and the Highlands

its scenery, Glencoe offers a good dose of bloody clan history. The visitors center has a fine exhibit with a 14-minute video about the massacre (50p, daily 9:30-17:30, shorter hours or closed off-season, just east of town on A82, tel. 018552/307). It tells about the "murder under trust" of 1692, when the Redcoats massacred the sleeping MacDonalds and the valley got its nickname, "The Weeping Glen." For a good 1-mile walk, hike to the Devil's Staircase (trail leaves from A82, 8 miles east of Glencoe). For a 3-hour hike, ask at the visitors center about walking to The Lost Valley of the MacDonalds (trail leaves from A82, 3 miles east of Glencoe). For good pub food in the glen, try the King's Hotel on A82.

Many find Glencoe more interesting than Oban for an overnight stop. In Glencoe village, Arthur Smith runs the **Cala Sona B&B**. Aptly named "house of happiness" in Gaelic, he entertains his guests with a peat fire, ghost stories, and tales of the Glencoe massacre (S-£13, D-£26, on the main street, tel. 018552/314). Nearest TI is in Ballachulish (tel. 018552/296).

Ben Nevis—From Fort William, take a peek at Britain's highest peak, Ben Nevis (over 4,400 feet). Thousands of visitors walk to its summit each year. On a clear day you can admire her from a distance. Britain's only mountain cablecars can take you to the not-very-lofty 2,150-foot level (signposted on A82, £5, 10-minute ride, tel. 01397/705825).

▲Caledonian Canal—Three lochs and a series of canals cut Scotland in two. Oich, Lochy, and Ness were connected in the early 1800s by the great British engineer Thomas Telford. For a good look at the locks, see "Neptune's Staircase" where you'll find a park built along a series of about ten locks (2 miles north of Fort William, detour 1 mile on A830). Fort Augustus is another good lock stop. If you travel between Fort William and Inverness (60 miles), you'll follow Telford's work—20 miles of canals and locks between 40 miles of lakes, raising ships from sea level to 51 feet (Ness) to 93 feet (Lochy) to 106 feet (Oich).

Loch Ness—I'll admit it. I had my zoom lens out and my eyes on the water. The local tourist industry thrives on the legend of the Loch Ness monster. It's a thrilling thought, and there have been several seemingly reliable "sightings" (monks, policemen, and now sonar images). The Loch, 24 miles long, less than a mile wide, and the third deepest in Europe, is deepest near the Urquhart Castle. Most monster sightings are in this area.

The Nessie commercialization is so tacky that there are two "official" Loch Ness Exhibition Centres within 100 yards of each other. Each has a tour-bus parking lot and more square footage devoted to their shop than their exhibit. The first one (£4, daily 9:00-19:30) is a high-school-quality photo report followed by the 30-minute "We believe in the Loch Ness monster" movie, featuring credible-sounding locals explaining what they saw and a review of modern Nessie searches. The place closest to Inverness (in a big stone mansion) is a little better, with a 40-minute series of video bits on the geological and historical environment that bred the monster story and the various searches (£4, 9:00-20:30). The exhibits are fascinating, but way overpriced. The nearby Urquhart Castle ruins (£3, 9:30-18:30) are gloriously situated with a view of virtually the entire Loch Ness. It's an empty shell of a castle with crowds and parking problems.

▲**Culloden Battlefield**—Scottish troops under Bonnie Prince Charlie were defeated here in 1746 by the English. This last land battle fought on British soil spelled the end of Jacobite resistance and the fall of the clans. The visitors center makes the short detour worthwhile with a great exhibit, a stirring 16-minute audiovisual show every 20 minutes, a furnished old cottage, and the memorial battlegrounds (£2, daily 9:00-18:00, shorter hours off-season, good tearoom, tel. 01463/790607).

Inverness—The only sizable town in the north of Scotland, with 42,000 people, Inverness is pleasantly located on a river at the base of a castle (not worth a look) with a free little museum (worth a look, cheap café). Its Highland Music museum traces local music from heroic warrior songs to Gaelic rock (scan 6 hours of music for £3, Balnain House, Tuesday-Sunday 10:00-17:00, until 21:00 in summer, tel. 01463/715757). Check out the bustling pedestrian downtown and central TI (tel. 01463/234353). Inverness has good transportation connections. Nine trains a day link Inverness, Pitlochry and Edinburgh (3½ hrs), and buses run between Oban and Inverness (6/day, 4 hrs). For Sleeping in Inverness, see below.

Pitlochry—This pleasant tourist town makes an enjoyable overnight stop. Its Edradour Scotch distillery offers a free 1-hour guided tour, 10-minute audiovisual show, and of course, tasting (9:30-17:00, closed Sunday, 2 miles east of town, tel. 01796/472095). The Blair Athol Distillery (half a mile from town, 9:30-16:00, closed Sunday, tel. 472234) gives £2 hour-long tours (2/hr). Pitlochry also has a salmon ladder (jumping May and June, free viewing area, 10-minute walk from town) and plenty of forest walks. The town theater offers a different play every night. (TI, 9:00-20:00, tel. 01796/472215.) For Sleeping in Pitlochry, see below.

Sleeping in Inverness and Pitlochry
(£1 = about $1.50)
Sleep code: **S**=Single, **D**=Double/Twin, **T**=Triple, **Q**=Quad, **B**=Bath/Shower, **WC**=Toilet, **CC**=Credit Card (Visa, Mastercard, Amex).

Sleeping in Inverness (tel. code: 01463)

These rooms are all a short walk from the train station and town center. The first two are on a quiet street just up the steps from the pedestrian High Street.

Ardconnel House is tasteful, bright, spacious, and thoroughly classy (S-£16, D-£32, T-£48, family deals, TVs in rooms; 21 Ardconnel Street, IV2 3EU, tel. 240455, Mrs. MacKenzie). **The Holies** is much simpler, but still a fine value, with only three rooms and sturdy beds (S-£14, D-£28, T-£42, family deals; 24 Ardconnel Street, tel. 231291, Mrs. Proudfoot). The town **youth hostel** (£8 including sheets, up the street from the castle at 1 Old Edinburgh Road, tel. 231771, 6- to 20-bed rooms) and the much more laid-back **Inverness Student Hotel** (£8 per bed with sheets in one of its ten 6-bed rooms, across the street from the hostel at 8 Culduthel Road, tel. 236556) are cheap and central.

Sleeping in Pitlochry (tel. code: 01796)

Try **Craigroyston House**, a big Victorian country house with eight Laura Ashley-style rooms and a piano in the lounge, just up the steps from the TI and run by charming Gretta Maxwell (£16-£23 per person depending on the season, all rooms with private bath, next to the church at 2 Lower Oakfield, PH16 5HQ, tel. 472053). Mrs. Maxwell can find you another B&B if her place is full. Pitlochry's fine **youth hostel** is on Knockard Road above the main street (£7 bunks, tel. 472308).

Scottish Words

aye—yes	**inch, innis**—island
ben—mountain	**inver**—river, mouth
bonnie—beautiful	**kyle**—strait, firth
carn—heap of stones	**loch**—lake
creag—rock, cliff	**neeps**—turnips
tattie—potato	

haggis—rich assortment of oats and sheep organs stuffed into a chunk of sheep intestine, liberally seasoned, boiled, and eaten—mostly by tourists. Usually served with "neeps and tatties." Tastier than it sounds.

Route Tips for Drivers

Lake District to Oban (220 miles): From Keswick, take
A66 18 miles to M6 and speed nonstop north (via Penrith
and Carlisle), crossing Hadrian's Wall into bonnie Scotland.
The road stays great, becoming the M74 south of Glasgow.
To slip quickly through Glasgow, leave M74 at Junction 4
onto M73, following signs to M8/Glasgow. Leave M73 at
Junction 2, exiting onto M8. Stay on M8 west through
Glasgow, exiting on Junction 30, cross the Erskine Bridge
(60p), and turn left on A82, following signs to Crianlarich.
(For a scenic drive through Glasgow, take Exit 17 off M8
and stay on A82, direction: Dumbarton.) In a few minutes
you'll be driving along scenic Loch Lomond. The first picnic
turnout has the best lake views, lots of benches, a grassy
park, and kids' playground. Halfway up the loch, at Tarbet,
take the "tourist route" left on to A83, drive along saltwater
Loch Long toward Inveraray via Rest-and-Be-Thankful Pass.
(This colorful name comes from the 1880s, when second-
and third-class coach passengers got out and pushed the
coach and first-class passengers up the hill.) Stop in
Inveraray, a lovely castle-town on Loch Fyne. Park near the
pier. How's the fishing? The town jail, now an entertaining
museum, is a "19th-century living prison" (£4, daily 9:30-
18:00, last admission 17:00, tel. 01499/2381). Leaving
Inveraray, drive through a gate (at the Woolen Mill) to
A819, through Glen Aray, and along scenic Loch Awe.
A85 takes you into Oban.

**Oban to Glencoe (45 miles) to Loch Ness (75 miles) to
Inverness (20 miles) to Edinburgh (150 miles):** Barring
traffic, you'll make great time on good, mostly two-lane
roads. Americans are generally timid about passing. Study
the British. Be careful, but if you don't pass, diesel fumes and
large trucks might be your memory of this drive. From Oban,
follow the coastal A828 toward Fort William. At Loch Leven
and Ballachulish village, leave A828, taking A82 into Glencoe.
Drive through the village into the valley for 10 minutes for a
grand view of the vast Rannoch Moor. Then make a U-turn
and return through the valley. Continue north on A82, over
the bridge, past Fort William toward Loch Ness. Follow the
Caledonian Canal on A82 for 60 miles, stopping at Loch
Ness then continuing on A82 to Inverness.

Leaving Inverness, follow signs to A9 (south, direction: Perth). Just as you leave Inverness, detour 4 miles east off A9 on B9006 to visit the Culloden Battlefield Visitors Centre. Back on A9, it's a wonderfully speedy and very scenic highway (A9, M90, A90) all the way to Edinburgh. If traffic is light and your foot is heavy, you can drive from Inverness to Edinburgh in 3 hours.

For a scenic shortcut, head north only as far as Glencoe (Loch Ness is not much to see), then cut over to Edinburgh via Rannoch Moor and Tyndrum.

APPENDIX

Ireland

Ireland is small, about 150 miles by 200 miles, and it has no English-style motorways. Transportation is slow. Approach every trip as a joyride. Traveling in Ireland is generally cheaper than in England. The Irish pound is worth a little less than the British pound.

Ireland's B&Bs are even cozier and less expensive than England's, and traveling without reservations is not difficult. There are several good guidebooks on Ireland (such as *Let's Go: Ireland*). Ireland's weather ranges from damp to drizzly to downpour, and her people are her main attraction. You can't enjoy Ireland without enjoying the Irish.

Planning Your Time

A visit of two or three days isn't really worth the time and expense to get there. I'd plan on a minimum of five days or nothing at all. With two weeks, I'd follow the route on this map.

Getting Around Ireland

Irish trains are expensive and not extensive, with meager schedules and coverage. BritRail passes don't work here. The bus is cheaper and has more extensive routes; consider special bus passes. Students get a 50 percent discount with ISIC cards. Taking a car from England is complicated and expensive. It's better to drop your car in England or Wales and pick up a new one when you're ready to leave Dublin. Many hitchhikers find Ireland easy to get around in, safe, and very friendly.

If you're touring Britain and Ireland, consider an "open-jaws" flight plan, flying into London and home from Ireland. If you'll be touring the Continent with a Eurailpass, start it in Ireland (it's good on Irish trains and many buses) and ride free on the otherwise-expensive 24-hour boat ride to France.

Sights—Ireland

Dublin—Dublin, worth a day or two, crowds around O'Connell Street Bridge and the River Liffey. Boats land at nearby Dun Laoghaire with good bus connections into Dublin. (TI, 8:30-18:00, closed Sunday, has a room-finding service, 14 Upper O'Connell Street, tel. 1/8747733.)

Orient yourself by taking a city walking tour (ask at the TI). Visit Trinity College, notable for its stately grounds, historic buildings, and illuminated Book of Kells manuscript. The National Museum highlights the moving Nathan Hale-type patriotism of the martyrs of the 1916 Rebellion, and displays impressive medieval and earlier Irish artifacts. The Kilmainham Jail, symbol of the Irish struggle against Britain, contains martyr memorabilia. For something entirely different, tour the Guinness Brewery (Monday-Friday 10:00-17:00, video show, free beer).

For entertainment, sample the great Irish theater (Abbey Theater and many others, shows Monday-Saturday, 20:00), seek out some Irish folk music in a local pub, or check out Irish sports—hurling (the rugged national sport that's like airborne hockey with no injury time-outs) or Gaelic football (a violent form of rugby). Games are held nearly every Sunday at Dublin's Croke Park. Use the periodical entertainment guide called *In Dublin* for music, theater, sports, and tour listings.

Glendalough—The best short day-trip from Dublin for a sample of rural Ireland is a visit to Glendalough in the Wicklow mountains. Fifteen hundred years ago, the hermit St. Kevin established a thriving monastic school here. Today its ruins, surrounded by scenic forests and lakes, are understandably popular with tourists. Look into a one-day tour from Dublin.
Belfast—A direct 3-hour train ride north of Dublin, the capital of the North offers a safe, fascinating look at "The Troubles." Passing the checkpoint, you'll step into the traffic-free "safe zone." Browse through a bomb-damage clearance sale. Take a side trip south to the wonderful Cultra Open-Air Folk Museum; talk to the people. Check out the positive and creative way Belfast is splicing together its Protestant and Catholic young people. By riding a shared taxi up Falls Road into a working-class Catholic neighborhood, you can get a look at some powerful street mural art and visit the national cemetery. With a little common sense (don't sing Catholic songs in Protestant pubs), Belfast is as safe as London. (See the chapter on Belfast in my book, *Europe Through the Back Door*.) Belfast-Glasgow bus-ferry connections are great.
Cork—Ireland's rough but pleasant second city is visited mostly for the nearby Blarney Castle with its too-famous Blarney Stone. Hordes of visiting Americans smother it with kisses to get the "gift of gab"; local guys pee on it to get the gift of hilarity.
Cashel—This stirring religious and political center dates back to the mysterious days of St. Patrick. Fine Celtic-cross graveyard, good tours (2 buses daily from Dublin and Cork).
Dingle Peninsula—My favorite scenery in the British Isles is Ireland's West Coast, and the best in the west is the rugged beauty of hearty Dingle Peninsula, just north of the very touristy Ring of Kerry. Dingle is a Gaeltacht—a region where the locals still speak the old Irish or Gaelic language. This is a cultural preserve with traditional dress, music, and lifestyles complementing the natural beauty. (See the *Europe Through the Back Door* chapter on Dingle.) Train to the pleasant town of Tralee, then bus or thumb to Dingle town. Set up at Mrs. Farrell's Corner House (S-£14, D-£28, Dykegate Street, tel. 066/51516) or Paddy Fenton's Ballintaggert House Hostel (£6 beds, tel. 066/51454) on

the Tralee road just east of town. Rent a bike for the circular trip out to Slea Head (closest point to the U.S.A., incredible scenery, villages; explore the medieval monks' stone beehive huts, or *clochans*, along the way), but be home in time to catch the nightly folk music at O'Flaherty's Pub. Moran's Slea Head Tours are the best way to explore Dingle peninsula without your own car. John Moran minibuses small groups for 3 hours (£6, 14:15, not Sunday, many morning departures in July and August, tel. 066/51155, fax 51553).

Galway—The largest city in western Ireland, coastal Galway is cozy, historic, and 3 hours by train from Dublin and Cork (direct bus service to Rosslare, a ferry port). There are daily boats and cheap flights to the Aran Islands.

Aran Islands—Off the coast of Galway, this tiny group of wave-whipped islands is a stark, stubborn outpost of old Irish culture and not terribly touristy. Spend a day on the main island, rent a bike, and explore. Boats connect islands with the mainland. One goes to Doolin, home of Ireland's best folk music but not much else.

Donegal—Ireland in the extreme, Donegal is the cultural Yukon of this lush island, where everyone seems to be typecast for an Irish movie. Enter Donegal with caution—for while it has no real "sights," it *is* seductive, and many unwary visitors end up skipping the rest of their itinerary.

Connections Between Britain and Ireland

Prices on planes, trains, buses and boats vary with the season. Round-trips, Monday-Thursday departures, stays over a Saturday, and tickets bought 7 days in advance are usually cheaper.

Glasgow and Belfast: Scotland's Glasgow has great bus-ferry-bus connections with its sister city, Belfast (10-12 hrs, £20).

Holyhead and Dun Laoghaire: Boats sail between the Welsh port of Holyhead and the Irish port of Dun Laoghaire (pronounced "dun-leer-ee") three or four times a day (£18-£25, 3½ hours, get ticket ASAP in London, special deal for car plus five passengers for around £120).

London and Dublin: The London-Dublin 10-hour train/boat ride costs about £50, overnight or all day. The London-Dublin 12-hour bus trip costs £32 one-way or round-trip. Flights from London to Dublin and Belfast are fairly cheap (£95 regular one-way, £60 round-trip when purchased a week in advance and staying over Saturday, £34 one-way for those under 26) and easy to arrange at a London travel agency.

What's So Great About Britain?

Regardless of the revolution we had 200 years ago, Americans "go home" to Britain. This most popular tourist destination has a strange influence and power over us.

Britain is small—about the size of Uganda (or Idaho)—600 miles tall and 300 miles at its widest. Its highest mountain is 4,400 feet—a foothill by our standards. The population is a quarter of the U.S.A.'s. Politically and economically, Great Britain is closing out the 20th century only a weak shadow of the days when it boasted, "The sun never sets on the British Empire."

At one time, Britain owned one-fifth of the world and accounted for more than half the planet's industrial output. Today, the Empire is down to token and troublesome scraps such as the Falklands and Northern Ireland, Great Britain's industrial production is about 5 percent of the world's total, and Italy has a higher per capita income.

Still, Britain is a world leader. Her heritage, her culture, and her people cannot be measured in traditional units of power. The United Kingdom is a union of four countries—England, Wales, Scotland, and Northern Ireland. Cynics call it an English Empire ruled by London, and there is some tension between the dominant Anglo-Saxon English (46 million) and their Celtic brothers (10 million).

In the Dark Ages, the Angles moved into this region from Europe, pushing the Celtic inhabitants to the undesirable fringe of the islands. The Angles settled in Angle-land (England), while the Celts made do in Wales, Scotland, and Ireland.

Today Wales, with 2 million people, struggles along with a terrible economy, dragged down by the depressed mining industry. A great deal of Welsh pride is apparent in the local music and the bilingual signs—some with the English spray-painted out. Fifty thousand people speak Welsh.

Scotland is big, accounting for one-third of Great Britain's land area, but sparsely inhabited, with only 5 million people. Only about 80,000 speak Gaelic, but the Scots enjoy a large measure of autonomy with their separate Church of Scotland, their own legal system, and Scottish currency (interchangeable with the British).

Ireland is divided. Most of it is the completely independent and Catholic Republic of Ireland. The top quarter is Northern Ireland—ruled from London. Long ago, the Protestant English and Scots moved into the north, the (most Catholic and) industrial heartland of Ireland, and told the Catholic Irish to "go to Hell or go to Connemara." The Irish moved to the bleak and less productive parts of the island, like Connemara, and the seeds of today's "Troubles" were planted. There's no easy answer or easy blame, but the island has struggled—its population is only one-third (3 million) of what it used to be—and the battle continues.

As a visitor today, you'll see a politically polarized England. The Conservatives, proponents of Victorian values—community, family, hard work, thrift, and trickle-down economics—are taking a Reaganesque approach to Britain's serious problems. The Labor and Liberal parties see an almost irreparable breakup of the social service programs so dear to them and so despised by those with more than their share to conserve.

Basic British History for the Traveler

When Julius Caesar landed on the misty and mysterious isle of Britain in 55 B.C., England entered the history books. The primitive Celtic tribes he conquered were themselves invaders, who had earlier conquered the even more mysterious people who built Stonehenge long before.

The Romans built towns and roads and established their capital at "Londinium." The Celtic natives, consisting of Gaels, Picts, and Scots, were not subdued so easily in Scotland and Wales, so the Romans built Hadrian's Wall near the Scottish border to keep invading Scots out. Even today, the Celtic language and influence are strongest in these far reaches of Britain. As Rome fell, so fell Roman Britain—a victim of invaders and internal troubles. Barbarian tribes from Germany and Denmark called Angles and Saxons swept through the southern part of the island, establishing Angle-land. These were the days of the real King Arthur, possibly a Christianized Roman general fighting valiantly, but in vain, against invading barbarians. The island was plunged into 500 years of Dark Ages—wars, plagues, and poverty—lit only by the dim candle of a few learned Christian monks and missionaries trying to convert the barbarians.

Modern England began with yet another invasion. William the Conqueror and his Norman troops crossed the channel from France in 1066. William crowned himself king in Westminster Abbey (where all subsequent coronations would take place) and began building the Tower of London. French-speaking Norman kings ruled the country for two centuries. Then the country suffered through two centuries of civil wars, with various noble families vying for the crown. In one of the most bitter feuds, the York and Lancaster families fought the War of the Roses, so-called because of the white and red flowers the combatants chose as their symbols. Battles; intrigues; kings, nobles, and ladies imprisoned and executed in the Tower—it's a wonder the country survived its rulers.

England was finally united by the "third-party" Tudor family. Henry VIII, a Tudor, was England's Renaissance king. He was handsome, athletic, highly-sexed, a poet, a scholar, and a musician. He was also arrogant, cruel, gluttonous, and paranoid. He went through six wives in forty years, divorcing, imprisoning, or beheading them when they no longer suited his needs. Henry "divorced" England from the Catholic Church, establishing the Protestant Church of England (the Anglican Church) and setting in motion years of religious squabbles. He also "dissolved" the monasteries, leaving just the shells of many formerly glorious abbeys dotting the countryside.

Henry's daughter, Queen Elizabeth I, made England a great naval and trading power and presided over the Elizabethan era of great writers, including Shakespeare.

The long-standing quarrel between England's "divine right" kings and nobles in Parliament finally erupted into a Civil War (1643). Parliament forces under the Puritan farmer Oliver Cromwell defeated—and de-headed—King Charles I. This Civil War left its mark on much of what you'll see in England. Eventually, Parliament invited

Charles' son to retake the throne. This restoration of the monarchy was accompanied by a great rebuilding of London (including Christopher Wren's St. Paul's Cathedral), which had been devastated by the Great Fire of 1666.

Britain grew as a naval superpower, colonizing and trading with all parts of the globe. Her naval superiority ("Britannia rules the waves") was secured by Admiral Nelson's victory over Napoleon's fleet at the Battle of Trafalgar, while Lord Wellington stomped Napoleon on land at Waterloo. Nelson and Wellington are memorialized by many arches, columns, and squares throughout England.

Economically, Britain led the world into the Industrial Age with her mills, factories, coal mines, and trains. By the time of Queen Victoria's reign (1837–1901), Britain was at the zenith of power with a colonial empire that covered one-fifth of the world. The 20th century has not been kind to Britain, however. Two World Wars devastated the population. The Nazi Blitz reduced much of London to rubble. Her colonial empire has dwindled to almost nothing, and she is no longer an economic superpower. The "Irish Troubles" are a constant thorn as the Catholic inhabitants of British-ruled Northern Ireland fight for the same independence their southern neighbors won decades ago. The war over the Falkland Islands in 1982 showed how little of the British Empire is left, but also how determined the British are to hang onto what remains.

But the tradition (if not the substance) of greatness continues, presided over by Queen Elizabeth II, her husband Prince Philip, the heir-apparent Prince Charles, and a distant relative—his wife, Princess Diana. With economic problems, the separation of Charles and Diana, the Fergie fiasco, and a relentless popular press, the royal family is having a tough time. But the queen has stayed above the mess and most British people still jump at an opportunity to see royalty. American onlookers should remember that royal marriages have historically been disasters. The problems of Charles and Diana seem unprecedented only because they follow the unusually happy married lives of Queen Elizabeth and her mother. Britain remains a constitutional monarchy.

Britain's Royal Families

800–1066	Saxon and Danish kings
1066–1150	Norman invasion, Norman kings
1150–1400	Plantagenets
1400–1460	Lancaster
1460–1485	York
1485–1600	Tudor (Henry VIII, Elizabeth I)
1600–1649	Stuart (with civil war and beheading of Charles I)
1649–1660	Commonwealth, Cromwell, no royal head of state
1660–1700	Stuart restoration of monarchy
1700–1900	Hanover (four Georges, Victoria)
1900–1910	Edward VII
1910–present	House of Windsor (George V, Edward VII, George VI, Elizabeth II)

Architecture in Britain

From Stonehenge to Big Ben, travelers are storming castle walls, climbing spiral staircases, and snapping the pictures of 5,000 years of architecture. Let's sort it out.

The oldest stuff—mysterious and prehistoric—goes from before Roman times back to 3000 B.C. The earliest—such as Stonehenge and Avebury—is from the Stone and Bronze Ages. The remains from this period are made of huge stones or mounds of earth, even manmade hills, and were built as celestial calendars and for worship or burial. Iron Age people (600 B.C. to A.D. 50) left us desolate stone forts. The Romans thrived in Britain from A.D. 50 to 400, building cities, walls, and roads. Evidence of Roman greatness can be seen in lavish villas with ornate mosaic floors, temples uncovered beneath great English churches, and Roman stones in medieval city walls. Roman roads sliced across the island in straight lines. Today, unusually straight rural roads are very likely laid directly on ancient Roman roads.

Roman Britain crumbled in the fifth century, and there was little building in Dark-Ages (Anglo-Saxon) England. Architecturally, the light was switched on with the Norman Conquest in 1066. As William earned his title "the

Conqueror," he built churches and castles in the European Romanesque style.

English Romanesque is called "Norman" (1066–1200). Norman churches had round arches, thick walls, and small windows. Durham Cathedral and the Chapel of St. John in the Tower of London are typical Norman churches. The Tower of London, with its square keep, small windows, and spiral stone stairways, is a typical Norman castle. You'll see plenty of Norman castles—all built to secure the conquest of these invaders from Normandy.

Gothic architecture (1200–1600) replaced the heavy Norman style with light, vertical buildings, pointed arches, tall soaring spires, and bigger windows. English Gothic is divided into three stages. Early English (1200–1300) features tall, simple spires, beautifully carved capitals, and elaborate chapter houses (such as the Wells cathedral). Decorated Gothic (1300–1370) gets fancier with more elaborate tracery, bigger windows, and ornately carved pinnacles, as you'll see at Westminster Abbey. Finally, the perpendicular style (1370–1600) goes back to square towers and emphasizes straight, uninterrupted vertical lines from ceiling to floor with vast windows and exuberant decoration, including fan-vaulted ceilings (King's College Chapel at Cambridge).

As you tour the great medieval churches of England, remember, nearly everything is symbolic. Local guides and books help us modern pilgrims understand at least a little of what we see. For instance, on the tombs, if the figure has crossed legs, he was a Crusader. If his feet rest on a dog, he died at home; but if the legs rest on a lion, he died in battle.

Wales is particularly rich in English castles, needed to subdue the stubborn Welsh. Edward I built a ring of powerful castles in Wales (such as Caernarfon and Conway).

Gothic houses were a simple mix of woven strips of thin wood, rubble, and plaster called wattle and daub. The famous black-and-white Tudor, or half-timbered, look came simply from filling in heavy oak frames with wattle and daub.

The Tudor period (1485–1560) was a time of relative peace (the War of the Roses was finally over), prosperity, and renaissance. Henry VIII broke with the Catholic church and "dissolved" (destroyed) the monasteries, leaving scores of England's greatest churches gutted shells. These hauntingly beautiful abbey ruins surrounded by lush lawns (Glastonbury, Tintern, Whitby) are now pleasant city parks. York's magnificent Minster survived only because Henry needed an administrative headquarters in the North for his Anglican church.

Although few churches were built, this was a time of house and mansion construction. Warmth was becoming popular and affordable, and Tudor buildings featured small square windows and often many chimneys. In towns where land was scarce, many Tudor houses grew up and out, getting wider with each overhanging floor.

The Elizabethan and Jacobean periods (1560–1620) were followed by the English Renaissance style (1620–1720). English architects mixed Gothic and classical styles, then baroque and classical styles. Although the ornate baroque never really grabbed England, the classical style of the Italian architect Palladio did. Inigo Jones (1573–1652), Christopher Wren (1632–1723), and those they inspired plastered England with enough columns, domes, and symmetry to please a Caesar. The Great Fire of London (1666) cleared the way for an ambitious young Wren to put his mark on London forever with a grand rebuilding scheme, including the great St. Paul's and more than 50 other churches.

The Georgian period (1720–1840), featuring the lousy German kings of England whom the celebrants of the Boston Tea Party couldn't stand, was rich and showed off by being very classical. Grand ornamental doorways, fine cast-ironwork on balconies and railings, Chippendale furniture, and white-on-blue Wedgewood ceramics graced rich homes everywhere. John Wood, Jr. and Sr., led the way, giving the trend-setting city of Bath its crescents and circles of aristocratic Georgian rowhouses.

The Industrial Revolution shaped the Victorian period (1840–1890) with glass, steel, and iron. England had a huge new erector set (so did France's Mr. Eiffel). This was also a romantic period, reviving the "more Christian" Gothic style. London's Houses of Parliament are neo-Gothic—just 100 years old but looking 700, except for the telltale modern precision and craftsmanship. Whereas Gothic was stone or concrete, neo-Gothic was often red brick. These were England's glory days, and there was more building in this period than in all previous ages combined.

The architecture of our century obeys the formula "form follows function"—it works well but isn't particularly interesting. England treasures its heritage and takes great pains to build tastefully in historic districts and to preserve its many "listed" buildings. With a booming tourist trade, these quaint reminders of its—and our—past are becoming a valuable part of the British economy.

British TV

British television is so good—and so British—that it deserves a mention as a sightseeing treat. After a hard day of castle-climbing, watch the telly over a pot of tea in the comfortable living room of your village bed and breakfast.

England has four channels. BBC-1 and BBC-2 are government regulated, commercial-free, and rather highbrow. ITV and Channel 4 are private, a little more Yankee, and have commercials—but those commercials are clever, sophisticated, and a fun look at England. Broadcasting is funded by a £70-per-year-per-household tax. Hmmm, 35 cents per day to escape commercials. Whereas California "accents" fill our airwaves 24 hours a day, homogenizing the way our country speaks, England protects and promotes its regional accents by its choice of TV and radio announcers. Commercial-free British TV is looser than it used to be but is still careful about what it airs and when.

American shows (such as "Roseanne," "Seinfeld," and "Home Improvement") are very popular. The visiting viewer should be sure to tune in a few typical English shows. I'd recommend a dose of English situation and political comedy fun ("Spitting Image") and the top-notch BBC evening news. Quiz shows are taken very seriously. For a tear-filled slice-of-life taste of British soap dealing in all the controversial issues, see the popular "Brookside," "Coronation Street," or "Eastenders."

And, of course, if you like the crazy, offbeat Benny Hill and Monty Python-type comedy, you've come to the right place.

Telephone Directory

City	Area Code/Number	
	Tourist Info	**Train Info**
London	no TI phone	928-5100
Bath	01225/462831	01272/294255
Wells	01749/672552	
Cardiff	01222/227281	228000
Stow-on-the-Wold	01451/831082	01452/529501
Chipping Campden	01386/840101	01452/529501
Stratford	01789/293127	0191/22302
Coventry	01203/832303	555211
Ironbridge Gorge	01952/432166	0121/643 2711
Ruthin, N. Wales	01824/703992	01492/585151
Blackpool	01253/21623	20375
Windermere	015394/46499	01228/44711
Keswick	017687/72645	01228/44711
Oban	01631/63122	63083
Inverness	01463/234353	01345/212282
Edinburgh	0131/557-1700	556-2451
Hadrian's Wall	01434/605225	0191/232-6262
Durham	0191/384-3720	232-6262
York	01904/621756	642155
Cambridge	01223/322640	311999
Dublin	01/8747733	366222

Other Useful Numbers:
Emergency: 999
Operator: 100
Directory Assistance: 192
Outside London:
London Directory Assistance: 142
U.S. Embassy: 0171/499/9000
International Information: 155
Lake District Weather Report: 019662/45151
Eurostar (Chunnel Info): 01233/617575
Train and Boats to Europe Info: 0171/834 2345

As of April 1995, all British area codes begin with 01. To update old British area codes: add a 1 after the 0. What was 071 is now 0171. This change goes into effect in April 1995. Until then, both new and old codes will work. After that you'll get a recording explaining the correct new code.

London Airports and Airlines

Heathrow
General Information: 0181/759-432,
Terminal 3: departures 0181/745-7067, arrivals 0181/745-7412
Terminal 4: 0181/745-4540
Air Canada: 0181/897-1331
American: 0181/572-5555
British Air: 0181/759-2525
SAS: 01426/931-301
United Airlines: 01426/915-500
TWA: 0181/579-5352.

Gatwick
General Information: 01293/535353 (for all airlines—American, Dan Air, Delta, Northwest, USAir, TWA)

Country Codes
International code: 00

U.S.A.	1	Germany	49
Canada	1	Italy	39
Belgium	32	Netherlands	31
France	33	Switzerland	41
Ireland	353		

AT&T "USA direct": 0800-8900-11
MCI "USA direct": 0800-89-02-22
SPRINT "USA direct": 0800-89-0877
"Canada Direct": 0800-89-0016
Note: When you call another country from Britain, begin your number with Britain's international code, 00.

Climate Chart

The chart below gives average daytime temperatures and average number of days with more than a trickle of rain.

	J	F	M	A	M	J	J	A	S	O	N	D
London	43°	44°	50°	56°	62°	69°	71°	71°	66°	58°	51°	45°
	15	13	11	12	11	11	12	11	13	14	15	15
S. Wales	45°	45°	50°	56°	61°	68°	69°	69°	65°	58°	51°	46°
	18	14	13	13	13	13	14	15	16	16	17	18
York	43°	44°	49°	55°	60°	67°	70°	70°	65°	57°	49°	45°
	17	15	13	13	13	14	15	14	14	15	17	17
Edinburgh	42°	43°	46°	51°	56°	62°	65°	64°	60°	54°	48°	44°
	17	15	15	14	14	15	17	16	16	17	17	18

Weights and Measures

1 imperial gallon   = 1.2 U.S. gallons or about 5 liters
1 stone   = 14 lbs. (a 175-lb. person weighs 12 stone)
British pint   = 1.2 U.S. pints
28 degrees Centigrade = 82 degrees Fahrenheit
Shoe sizes—about ½ to 1½ sizes smaller than in U.S.

British-Yankee Vocabulary

British/American
banger sausage
bap hamburger-type bun
biscuit cookie
bloke man, guy
bonnet car hood
boot car trunk
brilliant cool
candy floss cotton candy
cheers goodbye or thanks
chemist pharmacy
chips French fries
concession discounted admission
crisps potato chips
dicey iffy, questionable
dinner lunch
dual carriageway four-lane highway
fag cigarette
faggot meatball
first floor second floor

fortnight   two weeks
give way   yield
half eight   8:30 (not 7:30)
hoover   vacuum cleaner
iced lolly   popsicle
interval   intermission at the theater
ironmonger   hardware store
jumble   sale, rummage sale
jumper   sweater
knickers   underpants
knock up   wake up or visit
loo   toilet or bathroom
lorry   truck
motorway   highway
nackered   dead tired
nosh   food
off license   can sell take-away liquor
take away   to go
petrol   gas
pillar box   postbox
queue up   line up
randy   horny
ring up   call (telephone)
rubber   eraser
self-catering   accommodation with kitchen facilities, rented by the week
serviette   napkin
single ticket   one-way ticket
solicitor   lawyer
stone   14 lbs. (weight)
subway   underground pedestrian passageway
sweets   candy
telly   TV
to let   for rent
torch   flashlight
trunk call   long-distance phone call
underground   subway
verge   edge of road
wellingtons, wellies   rubber boots
zebra crossing   crosswalk
zed   the letter "z"

INDEX

RICK STEVES'

FREE TRAVEL NEWSLETTER/CATALOG

My Europe Through the Back Door travel company will help you travel better **because** you're on a budget — not in spite of it. Call us at (206) 771-8303, and we'll send you our *free newsletter/catalog* packed full of info on budget travel, railpasses, guidebooks, videos, travel bags and tours:

EUROPEAN RAILPASSES

We sell the full range of European railpasses, and with every Eurailpass we give you these important extras — *free:* my hour-long "How to get the most out of your railpass" video; your choice of one of my ten "Best of..." regional guidebooks and phrasebooks; and our sage advice on your 1-page itinerary. Call us for a free copy of our 64-page *1995 Back Door Guide to European Railpasses.*

BACK DOOR TOURS

We offer a variety of European tours for those who want to travel in the Back Door style, but without the transportation and hotel hassles. If a tour with a small group, modest Back Door accomodations, lots of physical exercise, and no tips or hidden charges sounds like your idea of fun, call us for details.

CONVERTIBLE BACK DOOR BAG $75

At 9"x21"x13" our specially designed, sturdy bag is maximum carry-on-the-plane size (fits under the seat) and your key to footloose and fancy-free travel. Made of rugged water resistant cordura nylon, it converts easily from a smart looking suitcase to a handy rucksack. It has padded hide-away shoulder straps, top and side handles, and a detachable shoulder strap (for use as a suitcase). Lockable perimeter zippers allow easy access to the roomy 2,500 cubic inch central compartment. Two large outside compartments are perfect for frequently used items. We'll even toss in a nylon stuff bag. More than 40,000 Back Door travelers have used these bags around the world. I live out of one for three months at a time. Available in black, grey, navy blue and teal green.

MONEYBELT $8

Absolutely required for European travel, our sturdy nylon, ultra-light, under-the-pants pouch is just big enough to carry your essentials (passport, airline tickets, travelers checks, gummi bears, and so on) comfortably. I won't travel without one, and neither should you. Comes in neutral beige, with a nylon zipper. One size fits all.

All items are field tested by Rick Steves and completely guaranteed.
Prices are good through 1995 (maybe longer), and include shipping (allow 2 to 3 weeks).
WA residents add 8.2% tax. Sorry, no credit cards or phone orders. Send checks in US $ to:

Europe Through the Back Door   ❖   120 Fourth Avenue North
PO Box 2009, Edmonds, WA 98020   ❖   Phone: (206)771-8303

Other Books from John Muir Publications

Travel Books by Rick Steves
Asia Through the Back Door, 4th ed., 400 pp. $16.95

Europe 101: History, Art, and Culture for the Traveler, 4th ed., 372 pp. $15.95

Mona Winks: Self-Guided Tours of Europe's Top Museums, 2nd ed., 456 pp. $16.95

Rick Steves' Best of the Baltics and Russia, 1995 ed. 144 pp. $9.95

Rick Steves' Best of Europe, 1995 ed., 544 pp. $16.95

Rick Steves' Best of France, Belgium, and the Netherlands, 1995 ed., 240 pp. $12.95

Rick Steves' Best of Germany, Austria, and Switzerland, 1995 ed., 240 pp. $12.95

Rick Steves' Best of Great Britain, 1995 ed., 192 pp. $11.95

Rick Steves' Best of Italy, 1995 ed., 208 pp. $11.95

Rick Steves' Best of Scandinavia, 1995 ed., 192 pp. $11.95

Rick Steves' Best of Spain and Portugal, 1995 ed., 192 pp. $11.95

Rick Steves' Europe Through the Back Door, 13th ed., 480 pp. $17.95

Rick Steves' French Phrase Book, 2nd ed., 112 pp. $4.95

Rick Steves' German Phrase Book, 2nd ed., 112 pp. $4.95

Rick Steves' Italian Phrase Book, 2nd ed., 112 pp. $4.95

Rick Steves' Spanish and Portuguese Phrase Book, 2nd ed., 288 pp. $5.95

Rick Steves' French/German/Italian Phrase Book, 288 pp. $6.95

A Natural Destination Series
Belize: A Natural Destination, 2nd ed., 304 pp. $16.95

Costa Rica: A Natural Destination, 3rd ed., 400 pp. $17.95

Guatemala: A Natural Destination, 336 pp. $16.95

Undiscovered Islands Series
Undiscovered Islands of the Caribbean, 3rd ed., 264 pp. $14.95

Undiscovered Islands of the Mediterranean, 2nd ed., 256 pp. $13.95

Undiscovered Islands of the U.S. and Canadian West Coast, 288 pp. $12.95

For Birding Enthusiasts
The Birder's Guide to Bed and Breakfasts: U.S. and Canada, 288 pp. $15.95

The Visitor's Guide to the Birds of the Central National Parks: U.S. and Canada, 400 pp. $15.95

The Visitor's Guide to the Birds of the Eastern National Parks: U.S. and Canada, 400 pp. $15.95

The Visitor's Guide to the Birds of the Rocky Mountain National Parks: U.S. and Canada, 432 pp. $15.95

Unique Travel Series
Each is 112 pages and $10.95 paperback.

Unique Arizona
Unique California
Unique Colorado
Unique Florida
Unique New England
Unique New Mexico
Unique Texas
Unique Washington

2 to 22 Days Itinerary Planners
2 to 22 Days in the American Southwest, 1995 ed., 192 pp. $11.95

2 to 22 Days in Asia, 192 pp. $10.95

2 to 22 Days in Australia, 192 pp. $10.95

2 to 22 Days in California, 1995 ed., 192 pp. $11.95

2 to 22 Days in Eastern Canada, 1995 ed., 240 pp $11.95

2 to 22 Days in Florida, 1995 ed., 192 pp. $11.95

2 to 22 Days Around the Great Lakes, 1995 ed., 192 pp. $11.95

2 to 22 Days in Hawaii, 1995 ed., 192 pp. $11.95

2 to 22 Days in New England, 1995 ed., 192 pp. $11.95

2 to 22 Days in New Zealand, 192 pp. $10.95

2 to 22 Days in the Pacific Northwest, 1995 ed., 192 pp. $11.95

2 to 22 Days in the Rockies, 1995 ed., 192 pp. $11.95

2 to 22 Days in Texas, 1995 ed., 192 pp. $11.95

2 to 22 Days in Thailand, 192 pp. $10.95

22 Days Around the World, 264 pp. $13.95

Other Terrific Travel Titles

The 100 Best Small Art Towns in America, 224 pp. $12.95

Elderhostels: The Students' Choice, 2nd ed., 304 pp. $15.95

Environmental Vacations: Volunteer Projects to Save the Planet, 2nd ed., 248 pp. $16.95

A Foreign Visitor's Guide to America, 224 pp. $12.95

Great Cities of Eastern Europe, 256 pp. $16.95

Indian America: A Traveler's Companion, 3rd ed., 432 pp $18.95

Interior Furnishings Southwest, 256 pp. $19.95

Opera! The Guide to Western Europe's Great Houses, 296 pp. $18.95

Paintbrushes and Pistols:

How the Taos Artists Sold the West, 288 pp. $17.95

The People's Guide to Mexico, 9th ed., 608 pp. $18.95

Ranch Vacations: The Complete Guide to Guest and Resort, Fly-Fishing, and Cross-Country Skiing Ranches, 3rd ed., 512 pp. $19.95

The Shopper's Guide to Art and Crafts in the Hawaiian Islands, 272 pp. $13.95

The Shopper's Guide to Mexico, 224 pp. $9.95

Understanding Europeans, 272 pp. $14.95

A Viewer's Guide to Art: A Glossary of Gods, People, and Creatures, 144 pp. $10.95

Watch It Made in the U.S.A.: A Visitor's Guide to the Companies that Make Your Favorite Products, 272 pp. $16.95

Parenting Titles

Being a Father: Family, Work, and Self, 176 pp. $12.95

Preconception: A Woman's Guide to Preparing for Pregnancy and Parenthood, 232 pp. $14.95

Schooling at Home: Parents, Kids, and Learning, 264 pp., $14.95

Teens: A Fresh Look, 240 pp. $14.95

Automotive Titles

The Greaseless Guide to Car Care Confidence, 224 pp. $14.95

How to Keep Your Datsun/Nissan Alive, 544 pp. $21.95

How to Keep Your Subaru Alive, 480 pp. $21.95

How to Keep Your Toyota Pickup Alive, 392 pp. $21.95

How to Keep Your VW Alive, 25th Anniversary ed., 464 pp. spiral bound $25

TITLES FOR YOUNG READERS AGES 8 AND UP

American Origins Series
Each is 48 pages and $12.95 hardcover.
Tracing Our English Roots
Tracing Our French Roots
Tracing Our German Roots
Tracing Our Irish Roots
Tracing Our Italian Roots
Tracing Our Japanese Roots
Tracing Our Jewish Roots
Tracing Our Polish Roots

Bizarre & Beautiful Series
Each is 48 pages, $9.95 paperback, and $14.95 hardcover.
Bizarre & Beautiful Ears
Bizarre & Beautiful Eyes
Bizarre & Beautiful Feelers
Bizarre & Beautiful Noses
Bizarre & Beautiful Tongues

Environmental Titles
Habitats: Where the Wild Things Live, 48 pp. $9.95
The Indian Way: Learning to Communicate with Mother Earth, 114 pp. $9.95
Rads, Ergs, and Cheeseburgers: The Kids' Guide to Energy and the Environment, 108 pp. $13.95
The Kids' Environment Book: What's Awry and Why, 192 pp. $13.95

Extremely Weird Series
Each is 48 pages, $9.95 paperback, and $14.95 hardcover.
Extremely Weird Bats
Extremely Weird Birds
Extremely Weird Endangered Species
Extremely Weird Fishes
Extremely Weird Frogs
Extremely Weird Insects
Extremely Weird Mammals
Extremely Weird Micro Monsters
Extremely Weird Primates
Extremely Weird Reptiles
Extremely Weird Sea Creatures
Extremely Weird Snakes
Extremely Weird Spiders

Kidding Around Travel Series
All are 64 pages and $9.95 paperback, except for *Kidding Around Spain* and *Kidding Around the National Parks of the Southwest*, which are 108 pages and $12.95 paperback.
Kidding Around Atlanta
Kidding Around Boston, 2nd ed.
Kidding Around Chicago, 2nd ed.
Kidding Around the Hawaiian Islands
Kidding Around London
Kidding Around Los Angeles
Kidding Around the National Parks of the Southwest
Kidding Around New York City, 2nd ed.
Kidding Around Paris
Kidding Around Philadelphia
Kidding Around San Diego
Kidding Around San Francisco
Kidding Around Santa Fe
Kidding Around Seattle
Kidding Around Spain
Kidding Around Washington, D.C., 2nd ed.

Kids Explore Series
Written by kids for kids, all are $9.95 paperback.
Kids Explore America's African American Heritage, 128 pp.
Kids Explore the Gifts of Children with Special Needs, 128 pp.
Kids Explore America's Hispanic Heritage, 112 pp.
Kids Explore America's Japanese American Heritage, 144 pp.

Masters of Motion Series
Each is 48 pages and $9.95 paperback.
How to Drive an Indy Race Car
How to Fly a 747
How to Fly the Space Shuttle

Rainbow Warrior Artists Series

Each is 48 pages and $14.95 hardcover.

Native Artists of Africa
Native Artists of Europe
Native Artists of North America

Rough and Ready Series

Each is 48 pages and $12.95 hardcover.

Rough and Ready Cowboys
Rough and Ready Homesteaders
Rough and Ready Loggers
Rough and Ready Outlaws and Lawmen
Rough and Ready Prospectors
Rough and Ready Railroaders

X-ray Vision Series

Each is 48 pages and $9.95 paperback.

Looking Inside the Brain
Looking Inside Cartoon Animation
Looking Inside Caves and Caverns
Looking Inside Sports Aerodynamics
Looking Inside Sunken Treasures
Looking Inside Telescopes and the Night Sky

Ordering Information

Please check your local bookstore for our books, or call **1-800-888-7504** to order direct. All orders are shipped via UPS; see chart below to calculate your shipping charge for U.S. destinations. **No post office boxes please; we must have a street address to ensure delivery**. If the book you request is not available, we will hold your check until we can ship it. Foreign orders will be shipped surface rate unless otherwise requested; please enclose $3 for the first item and $1 for each additional item.

For U.S. Orders

Totaling	Add
Up to $15.00	$4.25
$15.01 to $45.00	$5.25
$45.01 to $75.00	$6.25
$75.01 or more	$7.25

Methods of Payment

Check, money order, American Express, MasterCard, or Visa. We cannot be responsible for cash sent through the mail. For credit card orders, include your card number, expiration date, and your signature, or call **1-800-888-7504**. American Express card orders can only be shipped to billing address of cardholder. Sorry, no C.O.D.'s. Residents of sunny New Mexico, add 6.25% tax to total.

Address all orders and inquiries to:

John Muir Publications
P.O. Box 613
Santa Fe, NM 87504
(505) 982-4078
(800) 888-7504